ONE WEEK LOAN

SHIRE PUBLICATIONS

LIFE IN THE VICTORIAN COUNTRY HOUSE

PAMELA HORN

SHIRE PUBLICATIONS

Published in Great Britain in 2010 by Shire Publications Ltd,
Midland House, West Way, Botley, Oxford OX2 0PH, United Kingdom.
44-02 23rd Street, Suite 219, Long Island City, NY 11101, USA.

E-mail: shire@shirebooks.co.uk · www.shirebooks.co.uk

© 2010 Pamela Horn.

Every attempt has been made by the Publishers to secure the appropriate permissions for materials reproduced in this book. If there has been any oversight we will be happy to rectify the situation and a written submission should be made to the Publishers.

A CIP catalogue record for this book is available from the British Library.

Shire History no. 5 · ISBN-13: 978 0 74780 750 6

Pamela Horn has asserted her right under the Copyright, Designs and Patents Act, 1988, to be identified as the author of this book.

Designed by Ken Vail Graphic Design, Cambridge, UK and typeset in Bembo.
Printed in China through Worldprint Ltd.

10 11 12 13 14   10 9 8 7 6 5 4 3 2 1

COVER IMAGE
The hall and staircase of a Victorian country house. The influence of the Gothic revival can be seen in the arches at the entrance, and the variety of rich fabrics and collectables show the wealth and affluence of the owner. (Christopher Wood Gallery/ The Bridgeman Art Library)

PAGE 2 IMAGE
Waddesdon Manor from the south. It was built between 1874 and 1889 by Baron Ferdinand de Rothschild. Typically, despite being built in an earlier French style, it included the latest conveniences and technology, including central heating, hot and cold running water, and even an electric bell system. (Edifice/The Bridgeman Art Library)

ACKNOWLEDGEMENTS
I am indebted to the libraries and record offices in which I have worked for the help I have received, and to the National Trust for allowing me to quote from the Disraeli papers, which are deposited in the Bodleian Library, Oxford. I am also grateful to those who have supplied illustrations for the book. These sources are credited in the text. Other illustrative material has been provided by the author or the publisher from their own collections.

Shire Publications is supporting the Woodland Trust, the UK's leading woodland conservation charity, by funding the dedication of trees.

CONTENTS

Chapter One

THE COUNTRY HOUSE AND ITS OCCUPANTS

THE IMPORTANCE of the Victorian country house in rural Britain depended not merely on its size or on the impressive expanse of gardens and parkland that surrounded it, but on the life, wealth, interests and character of the owner – who was usually male. As a magistrate he dispensed justice, as a philanthropist he gave help to the needy, and as a political figure he took a leading role in national and local affairs. In many respects the country house embodied his own family's sense of identity and achievement, often serving as their home through several generations, and acting as a focal point in their lives and that of the estate. Such events as the birth or coming of age of an heir, marriage, or a death, were marked in the surrounding area by publicity which, in the case of joyful happenings, like marriages, led to general celebrations, with the ringing of church bells and the holding of dinners and dances for the tenant farmers and cottagers on the estate, as well as for the family and their friends. When American-born Jennie Jerome married Lord Randolph Churchill, second son of the 7th Duke of Marlborough in 1874, she remembered that on her first visit to the family's Oxfordshire mansion, Blenheim Palace, they were met at the station by local people, some of whom unharnessed the horses from their carriage. This they then hauled through the town of Woodstock to the Palace amid cheering onlookers. 'I confess I felt awed', noted Jennie as she entered the environs of the Palace, with its acres of parkland, large ornamental lake, and monumental house at the end of a tree-lined drive.

Because of the authority landlords enjoyed, autocratic owners could lay down rules for their tenants which regulated such matters as personal morality, church attendance, the cultivation of gardens, and the cleanliness of cottages. They might influence the running of the schools and of the church, as well as taking a major part in the organisation of military bodies like the Volunteers or, in the twentieth century, the Territorial Army. Wives and daughters from country house families played their part, too, by distributing food to elderly or needy people on the estate and discussing their problems in the spirit of a 'Lady Bountiful'. In early Victorian Cheshire, Lady Wilbraham of Delamere House joined with other ladies to establish a Provident Dispensary to give affordable medical treatment to labouring families. Some of her other initiatives were doubtless less welcome. On most Saturdays she drove round the cottages in a pony carriage with various gifts such as red flannel, soup, and puddings. But the basket nearly always contained a bottle of castor oil, which she freely administered, to the consternation of the recipients. In the 1890s the young Duchess of Marlborough recalled the wider responsibilities she had, too, such as

Opposite:
A young Victorian lady in an idyllic garden. (Mary Evans Picture Library)

Above:
Blenheim Palace,
Oxfordshire, from the
south-east, c. 1900.
(Images and Voices,
Oxfordshire County
Council)

Right:
Sulham House, Berkshire.
The lodge and lych gate,
c. 1864, with the
lodgekeeper holding open
the gate. (Museum of
English Rural Life,
University of Reading)

Left:
The role of 'Lady Bountiful'. One of the duties of country house ladies was to visit the cottagers and listen to their problems and complaints (Punch, May 1905).

Below:
Mme de Falbe driving a horse-drawn carriage at Luton Hoo in the 1880s. For some ladies the ability to drive the horses themselves was an expression of their skill and independence. (Luton Museum and Art Gallery)

Right:
A family group at Warwick Castle in the 1880s, from the reminiscenses of the Countess of Warwick.

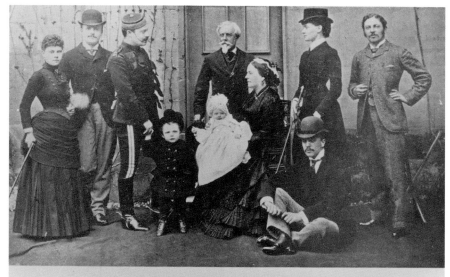

A FAMILY GROUP AT WARWICK CASTLE

Left to right standing: Lady Eva Greville; Col. Hon. Alwyne Greville; my husband; my father-in-law, 4th Earl of Warwick; myself; Hon. Louis Greville

Seated: My son, Guy; baby daughter, Marjorie; my mother-in-law, Countess of Warwick; Hon. Sir Sidney Greville

Below:
The first stateroom at Blenheim Palace in the early 1900s. A portrait of Consuelo, Duchess of Marlborough, stood in a corner of the room. (Images and Voices, Oxfordshire County Council)

attending agricultural and horticultural shows to present prizes, and addressing mothers' meetings and women's organisations, as well as arranging school treats in the villages bordering the estate.

It was with such properties in mind that in the early twentieth century a young footman, Frederick John Gorst, described the Welbeck Abbey estate where he worked as 'more like a principality than anything else; there were scores of people working beside me whom I did not know … Within the borders of Welbeck Abbey, His Grace the Duke of Portland wielded an almost feudal indisputable power.' At that date the staff numbered around 320 people, including fourteen housemaids and thirty-eight male and female servants in the kitchens and allied departments.

The freedom of the landed classes to take a prominent role in social and political life was made possible because others performed the domestic tasks necessary for their daily existence. Servants cleaned and maintained the richly furnished, often cluttered houses and cultivated the extensive grounds; they struggled upstairs with

Queen Victoria in the 1880s looking distinctly unamused!

heavy scuttles of coal for fires and cans of hot water for baths; they prepared elaborate meals, drove the carriages, and raised game for sport. Before guests, the menservants, in elaborate livery, symbolised the family's status and wealth, as well as providing the deference expected from social inferiors. 'The landed family', wrote one commentator, 'relied on its servants not only for its … comfort, but for its reputation.' At the same time the number of families in the upper ranks of society remained small for much of the nineteenth century. Indeed when it began, at a time when the wealthiest landowners were considered the richest men in the kingdom, the aristocracy formed a select group of just over three hundred families, many of whom were linked to one another by marriage or other connections. By 1885 the number of hereditary peers had climbed to nearly 450 and by 1914, partly as a result of the influx of newly ennobled financiers, industrialists and other businessmen, it had reached over 570. Most of these were in possession of country estates, with at least 1,000 acres considered necessary to support the lifestyle of a mid-Victorian landed gentleman.

One of the Duke of Marlborough's coachmen in elaborate livery at Blenheim Palace. (Images and Voices, Oxfordshire County Council)

A porter at the Great Gate, Blenheim Palace, in the early 1900s. The porters, like other male servants, had to be at least 6 feet tall. (Images and Voices, Oxfordshire County Council)

Sulham House, Berkshire, with a carriage and groom, 1866. (Museum of English Rural Life, University of Reading)

Importantly, however, the role that the aristocracy and gentry played, as well as the houses in which many of them lived, pre-dated the Victorian era. 'A well-regulated great family', optimistically declared the eighteenth-century literary figure, Samuel Johnson, 'may improve a neighbourhood in civility and elegance, and give an example of good order, virtue and piety.' In reality, it must be confessed that some of the more decadent and rakish characters in Georgian England, like Sir Francis Dashwood of West Wycombe Park and fellow members of the Hellfire Club, scarcely met this lofty ideal.

During the eighteenth century there was a major surge in country-house building and renovation. It came at a time of agricultural prosperity and when some of the most affluent landowners were also benefiting from Britain's industrial expansion and population growth. They were thereby able to exploit mineral reserves on their estates as well as to develop urban land. Already by 1790 grandees like the Dukes of Bedford, Devonshire and Northumberland could count on an income of over £50,000 a year. Their indoor domestic staff ran into at least thirty or forty people.

Much country-house construction, as well as the remodelling of older properties which took place at this time, was financed not out of income but out of the sale of outlying parcels of land on the estate or by an advantageous marriage. Henham Hall in Suffolk was built in the 1790s for Sir John Rous, later the 1st Earl of Stradbroke, through the sale of land in 1791 for £40,000 and by his second wife's dowry of £18,000. Marriage was also seen as a way out of other cash problems, both in the eighteenth century and later. In the 1790s, Lord Sefton hoped his eldest son would marry 'a fortune', to solve 'present difficulties' and to 'free the family from future anxieties'.

In a few cases nouveaux riches industrialists, merchants and financiers, benefiting from the new spirit of commercialism, began to build up estates, attracted by the

'Hold his head!' A groom expected to perform the impossible by an irascible employer (Punch, 1895).

prestige and influence that landownership conferred. The brewer Samuel Whitbread built Southill Park in Bedfordshire in 1795, while the Child banking fortune financed a country seat at Wanstead, designed along currently fashionable classical lines. Indian 'nabobs', gaining from sometimes dubious trading activities in the sub-continent, and West Indian sugar interests, benefiting from the slave trade, also played their part. The Lascelles family had already amassed a fortune through trading with the West Indies when in 1759 Edwin Lascelles commissioned Harewood House in Yorkshire. It was built on neo-classical lines, but Edwin, as an MP, spent much of the year in London. He and his wife sent instructions concerning the running of the estate to their steward.

One of the arches at Stowe House, Buckinghamshire. It exemplifies the preoccupation with classical architecture in Georgian Britain. (Country Life Picture Library)

Access to substantial financial resources was essential for the building of a country house and for laying out the gardens and parkland that surrounded it. At Blenheim Palace the high walls that skirted the property were, alone, said to have cost over £1,000 a mile.

The inspiration for the design of many of the houses was derived from Italy. In the eighteenth century the Grand Tour became an essential part of a gentleman's education, with Italy recognised as 'the fountain-head of artistic endeavour'. There the nobility and gentry could see for themselves the ruins of ancient Rome and admire the neo-classical villas constructed in the Veneto by the sixteenth-century architect Palladio. Despite doubts about the wisdom of trying to reproduce Italian-style buildings in an English climate, for much of the eighteenth century numbers of large houses were built to conform to this classical ideal. Unfortunately, to provide adequate heating for great halls with lofty ceilings and marbled floors through coal fires and charcoal braziers proved virtually impossible during the winter. Even in the 1860s an American visitor, Stephen Fiske, lamented the poor standard of heating. 'The English wrap themselves up to cross the hall as though they were going out of doors', he declared. This encouraged families to spend some of the coldest months in their London town house, where they could also meet their friends and take advantage of the pleasures, political activities, and entertainments that the capital had to offer.

The classical theme was taken up in the gardens and parks that surrounded the mansions, too, as at Stowe in Buckinghamshire, where statues of Greek and Roman

The Palladian bridge at Wilton House provided a further example of the popularity of classical architecture in Georgian Britain. (Richard Walker)

THINGS ONE WOULD RATHER HAVE LEFT UNSAID.

He. "Yes, I know Bootle slightly, and confess I don't think much of him!"
She. "I know him a little too. He took me in to Dinner a little while ago!"
He. "Ah, that's just about all he's fit for!"

Punch mocking the pretentiousness of those attending a London dinner party (1885).

gods, imitation temples, sham ruins and grottoes formed part of the landscaped park. Trees and water were seen as essential features by landscape architects in providing a proper setting for the Georgian country house, while gazebos and summer houses were used for the serving of refreshments. 'Classical forms', writes Dana Arnold, 'whether in architecture, painting, sculpture, garden design or literature enabled the expression … of a culture which aligned itself with Augustan Rome.'

Not all subscribed to this classical model, though. One of those who harked back to an English medieval tradition was Horace Walpole. His house, Strawberry Hill in Twickenham, begun in the 1740s, not only became over the course of forty years famous among his contemporaries, but proved to be a forerunner of a wider revival of the Gothic style of architecture. This was to become especially popular in the mid-Victorian years, including at Hughenden, home of the future Prime Minister Benjamin Disraeli. Under the influence of his wife, Mary Anne, this plain and undistinguished property was altered in the 1860s to conform to a neo-Gothic design. In September 1863 Disraeli proudly told a friend that they had 'restored the house to what it was before the Civil Wars'.

The Georgian enthusiasm for building led to alterations in the internal arrangement of houses, too, as regards both older properties and those newly constructed. The aim was to impress guests and to permit their free circulation between rooms at balls, assemblies and other social events. A number of rooms –

The greater informality of country house life before the Victorian era is suggested by this sketch of Testwood House near Southampton, c. 1830. Guests arrived unexpectedly when the household was in disarray, perhaps during spring cleaning. The sketch was the work of Mrs Sturges Bourne, the mistress of Testwood. (Hampshire Record Office)

saloon, library, drawing room and dining room – were arranged on a circuit so that they could be thrown open when entertaining. This enabled different activities, such as card-playing, dancing, quiet conversation and the serving of refreshments to go on simultaneously under the same roof and permitted the smooth mingling of guests.

At the same time the first moves were being made to reduce the pervasive presence of servants, who had to be close at hand to meet the wants of their employers or to carry out other duties. To this end back stairs and corridors were

A second Testwood House sketch showing Mrs Arbuthnot being greeted by the housekeeper, Mrs Smith, while cleaning activities continued around them. (Hampshire Record Office)

introduced for their use, while their quarters were often relegated to a separate wing, or to attics in the case of bedrooms for the maids. The introduction of an increasingly sophisticated system of bell-wires and bell pulls enabled them to be summoned as and when needed, rather than their having to hover in the vicinity of the family, waiting to be called and observing many of the family's most intimate activities. It was also seen as a way of instilling discipline into the domestic staff, at a time when footmen, in particular, were regarded as idle and self-willed, and below-stairs disputes among the servants added to the mistress's difficulties. In September 1769 an exasperated Lady Winn wrote to her husband to complain about the domestics at Nostell Priory, their Yorkshire home. Much of her time was taken up with hiring and firing staff and settling sometimes violent quarrels among them. She had to deal with gossipy, troublesome housekeepers who showed little sense of thrift and spoiled the junior servants, as well as impudent scullery maids who refused to milk the cows or to make the bread, and immoral goings on between the male and female domestics. According to her, they were having sex in each other's rooms 'twenty times a day'. Later on, Viscount Anson at Shugborough Hall complained of servants who would not bring up messages 'and always dispute who shall carry one … No footman appeared at coffee or tea yesterday evening or to make up the fire … The Evil has now got to such a height that Lord Anson expects soon to be left to wait upon himself … The more servants any gentleman keeps the more plague he has with them.'

Outdoor staff were always more independent than those working indoors. A disagreeable old gardener is engaged in digging up the croquet lawn, to the annoyance of the daughters of the house (Punch, 1867).

AN OBJECTIONABLE OLD MAN.

Young Ladies. "Going to make a Flower-Bed here, Smithers! Why, it'll quite spoil our Croquet Ground!"
Gardener. "Well, that's yer Pa's orders, Miss! He'll hev' it laid out for 'Orticultur', not for 'Usbandry!!"

The desire for increased domestic regulation and the separation of family from domestic staff were to be carried much further in Victorian times, when segregation and strict discipline could be carried to eccentric excess. The household rules of the aged 3rd Lord Crewe stipulated that housemaids were never to be seen by the family at Crewe Hall except in the chapel. Failure to observe this rule could lead to instant dismissal. A similar policy was adopted by the 10th Duke of Bedford, who died in 1893.

The changes in the structure of Georgian houses compared to their seventeenth-century predecessors were matched by the new and elegant furnishings installed in them. These included the introduction of mahogany and gilt furniture, the use of delicate porcelain, the purchase of expensive wallpaper, and the acquisition of carpets and chintzes. Paintings and sculptures were purchased on a series of Grand Tours, or items could be bought in by agents or at auctions. Many were housed in specially designed picture galleries. Anxious mistresses like Susanna Whatman, wife of a wealthy paper manufacturer, were concerned about the damage that could be caused to these valuable possessions by inexperienced housemaids. She issued a list of detailed instructions to them, requiring them to ensure that the painted chairs were not 'knocked against anything, or against one another … The books are not to be meddled with, but they may be dusted as far as a wing of a goose will go … in every room care must be taken not to open the windows with dirty hands. The locks in every room should be kept bright, the keys kept clean.' There is much more in a similar vein.

A well-conducted household added to a family's prestige. Augustus Hervey, for one, was deeply impressed by Lord Temple's Stowe, commenting admiringly: 'How well he is served … I never saw so large a house so well conducted, servants that have no … noise, but all attention and respect.' Not all guests, however, were so easily pleased. In 1826 the German traveller Prince Pückler-Muskau referred to the great expense involved in keeping up country houses, with their costly furniture, plate, elaborately liveried menservants, and profusion of dishes and wines served at the dining table. Then he added caustically: 'As long as there are visitors in the house, this way of life goes on … True hospitality [it] can hardly be called; it is rather the display of one's own possessions, for the purpose of dazzling as many as possible.' Nonetheless, ostentatious display remained a feature of many country houses into Victorian and Edwardian times, be they owned by aristocratic grandees or one of their nouveau-riche imitators. Mary Gladstone, whose tastes were comparatively simple, was sharply critical of Baron Ferdinand de Rothschild's Waddesdon, which she visited in August 1885:

> felt much oppressed with the extreme gorgeousness and luxury … pottered about looking at calves, hothouses, everything laid out with immense care, some rather cockney things, rockeries and such like … The pictures in [the] sitting room are too beautiful, but there is not a book in the house save 20 improper French novels.

A soulful-looking Mary Gladstone, c. 1880.

Young ladies exchanging confidences at a country house party (Punch, 1867).

Waddesdon Manor: the Aviary. (The Bridgeman Art Library)

In the eighteenth century, the interest taken in house design and renovation, and in the landscaping of parks, as well as the cultivation in hothouses of exotic fruits like pineapples, melons and grapes, encouraged an increase in country-house visiting by the affluent. They came not merely as guests of the owner but as tourists. Horace Walpole, for one, found that Strawberry Hill had become too much of an attraction.

In July 1783 he complained to a friend of the invading hordes, or 'the plagues' as he called them, who visited his house and were shown round by the housekeeper. 'I have no enjoyment of it in summer', he declared, since this was when his house was open to the public. The following year he sought to improve the situation by introducing personally signed admission tickets so as to limit the number of sightseers. He also drew up a 'page of rules' to be observed by those going round the house. Other popular properties adopted similar admission restrictions, while a few imposed fees, which were pocketed by the servants who showed the visitors round.

At Woburn Abbey, seat of the Duke of Bedford, sightseers in the 1780s were already being limited to Monday admissions only. At Blenheim Palace there were fixed fees, and when the Hon. John Byng went to Blenheim in July 1781 he complained of the high cost of the tour, adding drily, 'the servants of the poor D[uke] of Marlborough [were] very attentive in gleaning money from the rich travellers.' Eight years later a visit to the Duke of Devonshire's Chatsworth estate in Derbyshire aroused still greater ire. He resented having to tip the gardener in order to see the grounds and then:

In the conservatory at Luton Hoo in November 1886. The statuesque figure on the right was the Duchess of Teck, mother of the future Queen Mary, who was seated immediately in front of her mother. They were members of a country house party. (Luton Museum and Art Gallery)

*A summer picnic at
Sulham House in 1889.
(Museum of English
Rural Life, University of
Reading)*

The housekeeper next took us in tow, and shew'd us all the foolish glare,
uncomfortable rooms, and frippery French furniture of this vile house …
To complete the French-hood, the oaken floors of the great apartments are
all wax'd, so that ice is rougher, and every step upon them is dangerous …
Hardwick House [a nearby ducal property] as a house of comfort is worth
a dozen Chatsworth.

As the eighteenth century progressed, tour books and guides appeared, to cater
for the tourists, with the most frequented venues, such as Blenheim Palace and
Stowe, having the largest selection of guidebooks. Kedleston Hall, another popular
house that was open to visitors from the time it was built in the 1760s, not only had
a guide book but a polite and attentive housekeeper, Mrs Garnett. She held the
post from 1766 to 1809 and her portrait was painted showing her holding a copy
of the guide to the house's contents.

In the nineteenth century the vogue for country-house tourism among the
nobility and gentry faded away. In part this was because the houses themselves were
less likely to be open freely to sightseers, as families came to value their privacy.
Where parks and gardens were open to the public in Victorian times it tended to
be the middle and lower orders of society who visited. Sometimes, following the
growth of the rail network from the 1840s, they arrived in organised parties. Once
the railway reached Rowsley in Derbyshire in 1849, the Duke of Devonshire
arranged with Thomas Cook for the running of summer excursion trains, and
within weeks large groups were arriving from nearby industrial towns, such as
Derby, Sheffield, Bradford, Leeds and even Birmingham and Leicester. By the end
of the century it was estimated that Chatsworth was entertaining 80,000 visitors in
a season. By then, according to Peter Mandler, it had become 'the most-visited
private house in England'.

AMONG THE TRITONS.
(*The Duchess of Stilton at Home—Small and Early.*)
Mrs. Minnow (*indignantly, to her husband*). "LOOK, LOVE! MR. AND MRS. STICKLEBACK, OF ALL PEOPLE! TO THINK OF THOSE STICKLEBACKS BEING HERE!!"
Mr. Minnow. "YES, LOVE! AND TO THINK OF THEIR BEING *THE ONLY PEOPLE IN THE ROOM WE KNOW!*"
[*Mr. and Mrs. Stickleback are saying precisely the same things of their old friends Mr. and Mrs. Minnow.*

Left:
The 'Duchess of Stilton' entertaining snobbish guests at an evening 'At Home' (Punch, 1885).

Below:
Members of the Shuttleworth family with musical instruments at 'Collyers', Steep, in Hampshire in 1886. (Hampshire Record Office)

Chapter Two

VICTORIAN AND EDWARDIAN HOUSEHOLDS

'WHEN I WAS A CHILD,' wrote Lady Cynthia Asquith nostalgically of the 1890s, 'the lives of all well-to-do families were benevolently ordered by a large staff.' Yet, as she also admitted, houses in those days were firmly 'frontiered', with '"Upstairs" and "Downstairs" being quite separate regions … and all the turmoil, stress and steamy odorous heat of cooking kept well battened-down below stairs.' Occasionally a mistress might choose to perform some light domestic chores herself, such as arranging flowers or dusting especially valuable items of porcelain, or even supervising the moving around of furniture. But these spasmodic interventions in no way affected the general day-to-day running of the home.

The clear division between family and servants within the household was one that the architectural writer Robert Kerr strongly supported. In *The Gentleman's House* (1864) he regarded it as essential that family rooms should be private, and that the servants' department ought to be kept as far as possible separate from the main house, 'so that what passes on either side of the boundary shall be both invisible and inaudible on the other … The idea which underlines all is simply this. The family constitute one community; the servants another.' It was a recognition of changes that had been under way from the eighteenth century and were to peak in the Victorian and Edwardian eras. This social distance might lead, in extreme cases, to employers like Walter Ralph Bankes, owner of Kingston Lacy, communicating with the servants only by notes. Then there were arrogant mistresses like Lady Londesborough, who not only forbade her footmen to look at one another in her presence or to speak except in their professional capacity, but she herself never spoke to any servant except the butler, Martin, and the old housekeeper, Mrs Selby. They conveyed her orders to the rest of the staff. It was part of the same process that employers sometimes allotted servants a standard name, such as John for the first footman and Mary for the head housemaid, no matter what their real name might be.

Alongside this there was growing emphasis on the importance of timetables and strict timekeeping in the running of the household. This affected the duties of the staff but also impinged on the daily round of all the occupants of the house. Gongs and bells announced times for rising, for family prayers – in which the servants were expected to join – and for the serving of meals. The way the restrictions influenced the lives of the family was recalled by Lady Randolph Churchill at Blenheim Palace:

> When the family were alone … everything went on with the regularity of
> clockwork … In the morning an hour or more was devoted to the reading

Opposite:
A butler and his mistress are inspecting the dining table in this advertisement for knife polish. (The Robert Opie Collection)

Two ladies reading quietly in the sitting-room at The Elms, Hartley Wintney, Hampshire in the late-nineteenth century. The photograph shows a cluttered interior, so beloved by well-to-do Victorians. (Museum of English Rural Life, University of Reading)

Below:
A large domestic staff employed by Mrs Noble of Park Place, Remenham Hill, near Henley, c. 1903. (Images and Voices, Oxfordshire County Council)

of newspapers, which was a necessity for at dinner conversation invariably turned on politics. In the afternoon a drive to pay a visit to some neighbour or a walk in the gardens would help to while away some part of the day. After dinner, which was a rather solemn full-dress affair, we all repaired to what was called the Vandyke room. There one might read one's book or play for love a mild game of whist. Many a glance would be cast at the clock, which sometimes would be surreptitiously advanced a quarter of an hour by some sleepy member of the family. No one dared suggest bed until the sacred hour of eleven had struck. Then we would all troop out into a small anteroom, and, lighting our candles, each in turn would kiss the Duke and Duchess and depart to our own rooms.

Below:
Three ladies in a drawing room, where reading, embroidery, and conversation would occupy their time (Pieter Christoffel Wonder, 1780–1852). (Christie's Images / The Bridgeman Art Library)

Right:
Cleaning the plate was a task that fell to the under-butler in many large country houses. (The Robert Opie Collection)

At Inveraray Castle in Scotland, Frances Balfour, a granddaughter of the 8th Duke of Argyll, remembered his exasperation if the dinner gong were an instant late in booming through the Castle. If that happened the footman throwing open the dining-room door would be likely to find the Duke standing in front of him, impatiently waiting to enter. At Kingston Lacy, the mealtimes of the family and servants, respectively, were displayed in the servants' hall, to remind domestics of their duties.

In other country houses, however, the routine was less rigidly enforced, especially when the family were alone, without visitors. Then the female members not only spent leisure hours playing cards and the piano but engaged in drawing and painting and elaborate embroidery. On fine days there was gardening and during the evening there was much reading aloud, perhaps from the current issue of *The Times* or from a novel. The writing of letters took up a great deal of time, with news of daily doings carefully retailed. Then there were pastimes such as the pressing of flowers and the collecting of ferns. Scrap books were assembled and, by the more serious minded, fancy work was undertaken for charity, such as the making of tobacco pouches and ornamental slippers for sale at bazaars.

Playing the piano was a common recreational activity for country-house ladies (Henry Dunkin Shepard, fl. 1885–99). (Chris Beetles/The Bridgeman Art Library)

For male members of the household there were discussions about the running of the estate or the preservation of game. In the library, books were read and hobbies pursued, such as the collecting of birds' eggs and butterflies, which were then carefully displayed in specially prepared cabinets. Photography was popular among some, especially towards the end of the nineteenth century, while for others,

A lady watering the roses at a time when gardening became an increasingly popular female pastime. (Mary Evans Picture Library)

The library at Aldermaston Court in the late-nineteenth century. The library was often considered to be a 'masculine' room in the house. (Museum of English Rural Life, University of Reading)

including Sir John Harpur Crewe of Calke Abbey, it was the breeding of prize livestock that became the prime preoccupation. Sir John's specialities were Longhorn cattle and Portland sheep, and the awards they won at agricultural shows, it has been said, 'were the only recognition that he sought'.

But the pursuit of these wider interests did not mean that the formalities involved in running a country house were ignored. Hence family members and their visitors were expected to appear for meals appropriately dressed and that could require several changes of clothes during the course of a day. They also entered rooms only at times that did not interfere with the servants' cleaning routine. For front-of-house staff,

Ladies sitting in the garden at Sulham, c. 1880. (Museum of English Rural Life, University of Reading)

A country squire engaging a new coachman (Punch, *1900).*

Squire (engaging Coachman). "ARE YOU MARRIED?"
Coachman. "NO, SIR. THESE 'ERE SCRATCHES CAME FROM A CAT."

especially the housemaids, most of the chores in the house's public rooms had to be completed before the family came down for breakfast. This involved very early rising by the staff. At one country house a member of the family remembered the housemaids moving 'with light nimble footsteps, like mice scuttling from one corner to another', as they hurried to complete their duties. They were expected to remain out of sight unless called upon by the ringing of a bell, and should they meet members of the family or guests in the corridors they were expected to show their subordination and unobtrusiveness by pressing themselves against the wall. 'Each group in the household had to maintain its status and behave in such a way that boundaries were not blurred', writes Jill Franklin. 'Rituals of deference, affecting language, deportment and gesture were observed between under and upper servants, all servants and masters, children and adults, gentlemen and ladies.' Staff who had spent their working lives in country houses were aware of these social nuances. Hence well-trained upper servants were sometimes hired by the nouveaux riches to give them guidance in the subtleties of domestic life in upper-class circles. Books of etiquette were published in increasing numbers in the mid- and late-Victorian years for the same purpose.

There was a strict demarcation of duties among staff in stately homes. Lady Randolph Churchill learned that if a fire needed to be lit she must never ring for the butler. If she did, he would politely but firmly tell her, 'I shall send for the footman.' Another commentator, Richard Dana, remembered that when he visited Lady Frederick Cavendish he made up the fire himself. The servant whose duty it was to look after the fires was away from the house, 'and though there were several other servants at hand … she said she could not ask them.'

Naturally there were differences between households. At the Yorkes' relatively modest Erddig in Wales every effort was made to emphasise its 'family' nature. Some servants remained for years, including one of the housekeepers, Mary Webster, who served from 1843 until her death in 1875. When she died her employers were surprised to learn that she had saved over £1,300. Some of the Erddig servants were the offspring of other estate employees, like Harriet Rogers, who rose from nursemaid to become a lady's maid and then housekeeper. She remained in close touch with the family after her retirement, up to her death in 1914. It was in such circumstances that Lady Jeune claimed optimistically in 1892: 'Our servants and we are all members of a large family, who cannot get on independently of each other.'

In the conservatory, c. 1875–8 (James Jacques Joseph Tissot, 1836–1902). (Christie's Images / The Bridgeman Art Library)

When they died some employers left annuities or other bequests to their servants. The 8th Duke of Bedford, for example, at his death in 1872 left his London housekeeper and his valet annuities of £40, while his coachman had an annuity of £30 and the head housemaid one of £20. In addition they and the rest of the servants were to receive sums equal to three years' wages, as well as any other pay due to them when he died. Pensions were awarded to long-serving employees as well, so that when the 9th Duke succeeded he had to pay out about £1,000 in pensions to thirty-two old servants on the Woburn Abbey estate. Again, the 4th Earl of Carnarvon of Highclere Castle left all the servants who had been in his employ a minimum of five years when he died in 1890, a legacy equivalent to one year's wages. This included some of the outdoor workers, too, such as the head gamekeeper, the head gardener and the stable staff. All his permanent labourers were to receive a dark grey coat, which they were presumably to wear as a sign of mourning.

Saloon at Highclere Castle, Hampshire, home of the Earl and Countess of Carnarvon. (Country Life Picture Library)

*Lady Frederick
Cavendish, the former
Lucy Lyttelton, in 1864,
the year of her marriage.*

*A mistress reprimanding
the butler for damaging a
bowl (*Punch, *1912).*

Mistress (to new butler). "OH, JAMES, I FOUND THIS BOWL CHIPPED AND CRACKED IN THE PANTRY THIS AFTERNOON."
James. "I AM NOT THE CULPRIT, MADAM; I *NEVER* CHIPS NOR CRACKS. WHEN I BREAKS I SMASHES *UTTERLY*."

"THE SERVANTS!"

Jeames. "WEL', I WISH MY OLD WOMAN WOULD MAKE HASTE! I WANT MY LUNCHEON!"
Chawles. "IF SHE'S GOT CHATTERIN' ALONG O' MY GALS, SHAN'T SEE HER THIS 'ALF-
'OUR, DESSAY!" [*Overheard and mentally noted by her Ladyship, who was close behind.*

But this kind of provision was by no means universal. Eric Horne, who claimed to have spent fifty-seven years in service with the nobility and gentry as a footman, valet and butler, summarised the bitterness felt by those treated inconsiderately by employers. 'Servants are looked upon as part of the furniture of the house,' he wrote; 'live furniture, nothing more. If the live furniture is in the town house and is wanted in the country house, or vice versa, it is simply moved there … A servant gets work, wages, something to eat and drink, a bed to lie on. If [he] expects anything else from the employer, he's a fool.'

'The Servants': the arrogance and idleness of footmen mocked by Punch in 1870.

It was the mistress's role to oversee the running of her domestic establishment and to ensure that the senior staff closely supervised their juniors, so that tasks were carried out efficiently. The checking of household accounts was another responsibility and those ladies who failed to keep a careful check on outgoings often felt ashamed. Lady Fanny Russell, for example, found difficulty in balancing the books and was often overcharged, and Lady Frederick Cavendish found her early efforts to control expenditure also difficult. A few months after her marriage she discovered to her

THE FESTIVE SEASON.

Mistress. "AND YOU MAY ALL OF YOU ASK A FRIEND TO DINNER, YOU KNOW; AND, SMITHERS, YOU CAN ASK YOUR WIFE."
Butler. "THANK YOU, MA'AM. I THINK NOT, IF YOU PLEASE, MA'AM!"

'The Festive Season'. Below stairs in a country house (Punch, 1883).

horror that during a two-month period she and her husband had spent £121 on housekeeping. 'This I *must* cut down', she noted in her diary.

Mrs Beeton compared the mistress of a household to the commander of an army. As such she must lead her staff: 'Her spirit will be seen through the whole establishment.' Any laxity on her part would encourage idleness, slackness and even petty theft, with provisions such as tea, sugar and butter, which were not easily traced, secretly purloined by kitchen workers and given to friends and relatives. For this reason cost-conscious employers, like Sir John Ramsden of Bulstrode Park in Buckinghamshire and Richard Benyon of Englefield House in Berkshire, took responsibility for the ordering of fresh stores. Even in the 1890s Mrs Dee, Sir John's housekeeper, had to ask him to order such small items as oil for the oil lamps and stoves, as well as soap and candles. 'We have just now two oil lamps & stoves on in the dairy burning, the cream freezes so the butter cannot be made without precaution', she wrote in February 1895. Sir John also checked up on the numbers dining at the house. That included the family, visitors, servants and 'extras'. These last included casual workers like the 'odd man' who helped in the laundry twice a week and was given two meals a day on each occasion. Waiters were brought in to supplement the permanent staff at this and other households when large parties or other major entertainments were arranged. They, too, received refreshments as well as pay for the services they rendered. At Blenheim Palace printed rules included the proviso: 'No garden men or milkmen to have their meals here.'

In a well-run household the mistress gave instructions to the senior staff after breakfast, so that the butler could return to his pantry to issue orders for the day to the footmen, while the housekeeper passed on instructions to the housemaids, the still room maids, and probably the laundry staff. The chef or cook would discuss the daily menus with his mistress and supervise the activities of the kitchen maids and

A servants' hall with its hierarchy of staff dining in what seems to be a relatively modest household. The butler headed the table and the housekeeper was on his right. On her right were the ladies' maids, c. 1900.

IN A SERVANTS' HALL : AT DINNER.

scullery maids. This was an era when good food was important to the upper classes. That meant that wealthy 'outsiders' could climb into High Society on the shoulders of a good cook. The recruiting of a French chef added a certain prestige to a dinner table. Separate meals had to be prepared for the children and for invalids, so it was small wonder the kitchen was a place of heat and bustle.

A cook featured in an advertisement for baking powder. Reminiscences suggest that most cooks were of a more uncertain temper than this picture indicates. (The Robert Opie Collection)

When there was entertaining to be done, such as the arranging of house parties, a mistress would confer with the housekeeper over the allocation of rooms for her guests and their servants, as well as planning how to amuse them. Housekeeper and mistress might also discuss the distribution of charity to needy families on the estate. In recognition of the former's importance in the running of the household she – and a female cook – would be addressed by her surname and given the honorary title of 'Mrs', whatever her true marital status might be.

In most stately homes the female staff would be headed by the housekeeper but in small establishments with only six or seven indoor servants, the cook might take on that role. The male staff would be headed by the steward or the butler, and these senior servants had underlings of their own. The still room maids did the bidding of the housekeeper, while Ernest King, in his first post as a hall boy in Devon, was required to wait upon the butler. 'I first learnt to be a servant by being a servant to the servants', he wrote, 'the table in the servants' hall to lay, the staff cutlery to clean and the staff meals to put on the table … My day's work also included cleaning all the windows in the house, all knives and all boots, the family's, the butler's, and any visitors'.'

The Drawing Room, Wickham Hall, Kent, 1897, with its multitude of possessions designed to impress visitors and demonstrate affluence. (The Bridgeman Art Library)

Ladies' maids, because of their close connection with the mistress and her daughters, were in a special position. Often they were the offspring of lower-middle-class families and had frequently served an apprenticeship in dressmaking and millinery before embarking on their career. They also had to be skilled hairdressers. The most sought-after ladies' maids, at least by the fashion conscious, were French or Swiss, the former being preferred on account of their greater vivacity and superior dressmaking skills.

The nursery staff, under the charge of the head nurse or nanny, formed a separate department and had little to do with the rest of the servants, unless the nanny chose to interfere. As the next chapter will show, a nurse or nursemaid was often closer to the children than was their mother, especially if the parents had marital problems or led an active social life.

These exceptions apart, the housekeeper was expected to direct the female servants and ensure that everything ran smoothly. That included looking after the linen and issuing the stores to her subordinates at regular intervals, as well as ensuring the maids did not leave the house without permission. At Englefield House there was the further proviso that they were to be 'dressed quietly' when they did go out.

At Longleat the Marchioness of Bath remembered the housekeeper performing 'feats of alchemy' in the still room, distilling 'rose water from dark damask roses … preserving fruits, making jam, candying peel, … drying lavender to keep the linen cupboard sweet, and forever harrying the still room maids'.

Among the male staff the house steward was supreme or, if no steward were employed, the butler filled that role. He also looked after the household plate and the wine cellar, while some carried out brewing, especially in the early Victorian years. He would normally wait upon the family at the main meals of the day. One of his most important duties was looking after the wine cellar, however, and this could lead to problems. At Cliveden there were five different butlers between October 1906 and July 1909. Two were dismissed for drunkenness, one because he was a 'bad manager', and one was sent away after six weeks because although competent he had 'too big an idea of his position'. The fifth remained and held office until 1920. In smaller households, like Flitwick Manor in Bedfordshire, the butler might have other responsibilities, too, such as delivering messages on his master's behalf or, as in July 1847, mending and refixing a lamp in the music room. He remained in the service of his master, John Thomas Brooks, from 1843 until the latter's death

The butler's traditional fondness for alcohol mocked by Punch *in 1873.*

"ON THE FACE OF IT."

Host. "I DON'T LIKE THIS LAFITTE HALF SO WELL AS THE LAST, BINNS. HAVE YOU NOTICED ANY DIFFERENCE?"
New Butler. "WELL, SIR, FOR MYSELF I DON'T DRINK CLARET; I FIND PORT AGREES WITH ME SO MUCH BETTER!!"

Althorp House in Northamptonshire, seat of Earl and Countess Spencer. (David Brown)

in December 1858. In Brooks's will he was left a legacy of nineteen guineas 'as a token of my kind remembrance'.

The responsibilities of Henry Thorpe, steward at Althorp, were of a different order, as is shown in a letter he wrote in January 1857 to his master, Earl Spencer. Thorpe was in his late fifties and his lengthy experience may account for the somewhat peremptory tone of the letter:

> As respects the Usher of the hall it is quite requisite to have a steady sober man in that situation … Without him there would be nothing but irregularity & waste – he is responsible for the time of the meals being properly kept, to see that the meat is properly cut & when done with carried straight to the kitchen, to serve out the ale as well as to draw it … at ten o'clock he goes to his room. Such my Lord has been the regulation & practise [*sic*] at Althorp hitherto … which I hope your Lordship will not alter … Under the above System, every servant has had a plenty of everything without waste or abuse for I have not seen a man drunk in the five years that I have served your Lordship's family … I yesterday took Stock of your Lordship's wine cellar and carried the amount to your Lordship's private stock book, it contains (with the exception of the American wines which I have Binn'd away) 9,043 bottles …

In later correspondence he referred to the need to appoint a new under-butler and footmen, as well as ordering fresh liveries for them.

At Blenheim Palace, Consuelo, Duchess of Marlborough, remembered the house steward's rule over the men was absolute. Next to him ranked the groom of the chambers, whose duties included keeping the numerous writing tables supplied with paper, pens and ink. He was responsible for dispatching mail from the house, ordering the newspapers, and ironing them before the family handled them. He performed much ceremonial door-opening and at meals helped with the serving. The footmen were the male servants most directly subordinate to the butler, and carried out various tasks, ranging from attending their employers in the carriage when making calls, to cleaning knives and boots, carrying coal, cleaning plate, looking after the lamps and candle-holders, waiting at table and answering the bell. With these varied duties and the long hours worked, a man might walk miles in a day up and down stairs and along corridors in a really large house.

It was part of the ceremonial ritual that footmen were expected to be tall, over 6 feet for preference, and that for much of the period they were required to wear elaborate livery and to have powdered hair, especially at important dinners or other major events. They were hired partly as symbols of the family's wealth and importance and their earnings were influenced by their appearance. At Blenheim Palace they

Above:
*The Duchess of Marlborough and her younger son, Lord Ivor Charles Churchill (*The Tatler, *1901).*

Left:
Blenheim Palace: the East Garden with a young gardener and an impressive view of the parkland beyond, c. 1900. (Images and Voices, Oxfordshire County Council)

received a powdering allowance of two guineas a year to enable them to purchase the Violet powder used in this process. Some wealthy families recruited 'matching footmen' in height and figure, to add to the general display. The French visitor Hippolyte Taine claimed that 'the ornamental look [was] worth to them as much as £20 a year', although he added sourly that their 'stuck-up airs have become proverbial'. For their part, many footmen enjoyed this 'theatre of service', dressing up and being part of the ceremonial. Unlike female staff, who had to provide their own uniforms, the livery and working suits worn by under-butlers, footmen and hall boys were provided by employers. Stewards and butlers did not wear livery, but might receive a clothing allowance in lieu.

The distinctions between upper and lower servants were reflected in their eating arrangements. Although in smaller households they would probably eat together in the servants' hall, in large establishments like Welbeck Abbey, Longleat, Blenheim and Hagley, home of the Lytteltons, the upper servants had their meals in the steward's or housekeeper's room. At most they would solemnly process into the servants' hall for the main course of the midday dinner, before returning to the housekeeper's room to eat their pudding. While they were present, juniors were expected to remain silent. At Welbeck the young footman Frederick Gorst remembered the senior staff – labelled the 'Upper Ten' – were waited on by two steward's room footmen when they ate in the steward's room. 'We, the Lower Five, ate our meals in the Servants' Hall … At Welbeck the upper servants adopted an arrogant attitude towards the under servants.' By the juniors, the steward's or housekeeper's room was called 'the Pugs' parlour'.

Senior staff, especially the housekeeper, the nanny and the butler, might remain in a family for many years. Some stayed on even after retirement, so that Mrs Guymour, the Carnarvons' long-serving housekeeper, resided at Highclere Castle

A house party in the drawing room at Luton Hoo, November 1886. M de Falbe, the host, was standing second from the left and Ida de Falbe was seated in the sedan chair. (Luton Museum and Art Gallery)

IN A REGISTRY OFFICE (MRS. HUNT'S, DUKE STREET, W.): SERVANTS SEEKING SITUATIONS.

Servants seeking situations at Mrs Hunt's registry office in London, c. 1900.

until her death in the early 1850s. Mary Morton, the former nanny, was allocated a lodge and had a fifteen-year-old maid to look after her. When she died at Highclere in her mid-nineties she bequeathed the whole of her small estate, valued at under £450, to members of the family, and the 4th Earl, one of her former charges, acted as her executor.

Among junior servants changes were frequent. There were several reasons for this. For those seeking to make a career in service, especially the menfolk, it was essential to move around in their early years to gain experience and perhaps promotion, with higher wages, or a post in a more prestigious household. Sometimes they merely wanted a change or wished to escape from uncongenial employers or fellow servants. At Cliveden, the female staff employed by the Astors between the autumn of 1906 and 1912 included a housekeeper, five and later six housemaids, two still room maids, two kitchen maids, one scullery maid, five laundry maids, a lady's maid, and for much of the period a woman cook. Yet these nineteen positions were filled by about seventy-three women and girls in the six years. Only the housekeeper remained through the period, although there were few changes in the lady's maid and the cook. Most rapid of all were moves among the housemaids, especially the fourth housemaid, with eight different holders of that position between October 1906 and May 1908. One died in post and her three immediate successors each left after a month, complaining there was 'too much work'.

Contrary to popular belief, well-to-do employers rarely recruited senior indoor staff locally. That was partly because of the high standard of skill and efficiency they demanded and partly because they did not wish to have family affairs discussed among the villagers. When fresh members of staff were recruited mistresses relied mainly on the recommendations of friends and relations, or vacancies might be notified to leading tradesmen who supplied the household. Some advertised in the newspapers or consulted specialist servant registry offices. The best known of these in the later Victorian era were Mrs Hunt's agency in London and Mrs Massey's, with offices in Derby and later London. Mrs Hunt claimed to supply 'tested job servants for anywhere in a few hours' notice', and for those wanting to interview applicants in person, rooms for the purpose were offered on the premises.

A few mistresses of country houses tried to better the prospects of some young cottagers by training them for gentlemen's service in their own household. They included Anne Sturges Bourne, who even set up a small servant training school in her Hampshire home, Testwood, in the 1850s. Her aim was 'to substitute good … training for the chance first places [girls] now get'. She approached friends on behalf of her protégées and was in turn approached by them. As she confided to her closest friend, Marianne Dyson, in 1853: 'Getting places & people to fit is one of the chief employments of life.'

Similarly the Countess of Carnarvon wrote to a friend on behalf of her cook in July 1846, when the household was about to be broken up so that the family could travel abroad for her husband's health. She wanted to find a good place for Elizabeth, the cook, who had been with the Carnarvons nine years: 'her Conduct is most excellent, & she is a *very good* Cook & trustworthy in the Extreme … I do grieve to part with her & with several others, for we really have a very nice set of Servants.'

Many senior members of staff were stern taskmasters with regard to their subordinates. That was, of course, what their employers expected of them, especially as a high proportion of the juniors were young and sometimes high-spirited. According to Eric Horne, 'whistling, singing and courting [were] not allowed in good places', although he admitted that the prohibitions were sometimes ignored. Courting was conducted surreptitiously, perhaps 'in the housemaids' cupboard, where they keep their brushes and pails'. Senior servants were expected to stop this happening.

Even within country houses, too, despite the relatively comfortable living conditions, problems of overwork and staff disagreements could arise. For mistresses, staff conflicts created problems. At Hughenden, the Disraelis' country house, on

Mr G. Herbert Morrell's coach outside Headington Hill Hall, Oxford, with his coachman, G. Herbert, and two footmen in attendance at the rear of the coach, 1885. The Morrells were a nouveau riche brewing family in Oxford. (Images and Voices, Oxfordshire County Council)

Gardeners at Palace House, Beaulieu, Hampshire, c. 1896. The head gardener was probably seated on the wheelbarrow, wearing a boater. (Hampshire Record Office)

19 May 1857, Cuthbert Richardson, the butler, was dismissed for fighting with the coachman. At their London home in Grosvenor Gate, Charles Newberry, the under-butler, who had been in their service for nearly three years, left 'after a great quarrel with Mrs Cripps [the cook-housekeeper]', on 13 December 1865: '(by his own desire). Threatened to blow her brains out if she did cook his potatoes.' But there may have been another reason for the dispute, for in September of the following year he secretly married Mary Mansfield, the Disraelis' housemaid, who had continued to work for them after he left. Interestingly, on the marriage certificate he gave his address as 1 Grosvenor Gate, the same as his wife, even though he no longer worked at the house. The clandestine marriage was revealed less than two months later, when he suddenly died of a throat infection, at the age of twenty-eight. He was then employed by Lord Heytesbury as an under-butler. At that time Mary, too, left the Disraelis' employ.

At Blenheim Palace in the 1890s the Duchess of Marlborough lamented the 'frequent difficulties' between the various departmental heads, which she had to resolve. Inevitably they impinged upon her other activities and caused her personal anxiety. There were regular disputes between the French chef and the housekeeper over the intricacies of providing breakfast trays. At Dalmeny House, one of the Earl of Rosebery's Scottish seats, the disagreements were between his agent and the female cook, Alice Slater. As a widower and a leading political figure, the Earl himself played no active part in the squabble. About four months after Alice was appointed, in 1912, she hotly refuted the agent's charges of extravagance: 'the words extravagance & waste are very serious to a Cook. I have been most anxious all along to keep things going satisfactorily & I certainly do not allow waste … I fed twice as many people last month as were fed in the corresponding month last year', presumably because Lord Rosebery had been entertaining more guests and their servants at Dalmeny. However, the complaints continued and by the spring of 1913 she had decided to leave the post.

Even at Erddig, conflicts occurred. 'I am having great trouble with the numerous servants', wrote the recently married Louisa Yorke, in July 1902. 'Some are too noisy, some too grand, some find the work too much. I wonder if I shall ever be quite

Right:
Household prayers were attended both by family members and the servants, as this Punch *cartoon suggests (1882).*

AN UNSEEMLY INTERRUPTION.

Eva (who has been told not to make a Noise during Family Prayers, which she attends for the first time). "NAUGHTY GRANDPAPA'S MAKING A NOISE!"

Below:
An advertisement for Cambridge lemonade was set against the backdrop of a tennis party. (The Robert Opie Collection)

THE CAMBRIDGE LEMONADE

"THE FAVOURITE"

CHIVERS & SONS L^{TD} HISTON, CAMBRIDGE

settled.' She also had problems checking up on household expenditure.

A number of families imposed religious restrictions upon the servants. It was common to require staff to be Protestants, if the employers were Anglicans, and at Erddig Philip Yorke himself conducted prayers in the chapel as well as playing the harmonium for services attended by the family and servants.

Masters and mistresses did not always welcome the pervasive presence of their domestics, even though they were happy for them to perform essential household tasks. At Blenheim, the young, American-born Duchess complained of 'an irksome form of surveillance' during the 1890s. 'In the house I was followed by a black boy Marlborough had brought from Egypt to be my page. In his Oriental costume and turban he looked picturesque, but he was a perpetual source of irritation, for his garbled messages in broken English caused endless misunderstandings … with a page in the house, a coachman or a postilion to take me for drives and a groom to accompany my rides, my freedom was quite successfully restricted.'

In many respects the Victorian and Edwardian country house formed a closed world, in which employer and servants were bound together in mutual interdependence, as consumers and suppliers of goods and services. It was a world under threat by the end of the nineteenth century, as the effects of agricultural depression and declining incomes caused some landowners to cut staff numbers, and as many younger people became reluctant to embark on a life in service, even in the comparative comfort of a country house. There was resentment at the limited leisure they were allowed, as well as the restrictions on their conduct, including on their encounters with members of the opposite sex, and the need to wear a distinctive uniform, which some of the girls at least felt marked them out as social inferiors.

William Lanceley, who rose from a hall boy to become a house steward, claimed that there were households that were put on a 'servant blacklist'. They included those where mistresses constantly found fault with their employees. He revealed that in his youth there had been two very large establishments that were always shunned. In one case this was because of the character of the mistress and the other because of the house steward. 'When once unrest gets into a house, it takes a long time to settle down', he declared. He warned, too, that in-house promotions could give rise to ill-feeling and jealousy among the rest of the staff.

But equally there were senior servants who took pride in working in prestigious households and in giving high quality service. The butler Charles Cooper felt he had 'accomplished something' when he saw 'a well-laid table covered with beautifully kept silver' and waited on 'people who matter'. Likewise Mrs Boyce, a former lady's maid, claimed that if potential employers were 'just money-made people, well, nobody wanted to go there, they didn't know how to treat a servant. It had got to be breeding … The good old aristocracy of England, they treat you as a jewel. So we're a lot of snobs … really.'

Mr Sponge at Jawleyford Court.

A formal procession in to dinner (1853), with liveried footmen and a hall boy in attendance. (Mary Evans Picture Library)

Chapter Three

GROWING UP IN THE COUNTRY HOUSE

IT WAS COMMON for upper-class wives in Victorian Britain to become pregnant during the first two years of their marriage, and particularly in the case of landed families there was pressure on them to produce a male heir as soon as possible. The aim was to ensure the succession of the estate to the next generation. Daughters were less welcome. Tina Lucy of Charlecote Park, Warwickshire, was devastated when in March 1870 she gave birth to a third daughter. According to her formidable mother-in-law, Mary Elizabeth Lucy, she 'could not … be reconciled to her disappointment that this new baby was not a boy. She kept crying and saying, "Oh! What will Spencer [her husband] say to me for having another girl".' In the event the Lucys did not have a son and when Spencer died the estate passed to another branch of the family. At Kingston Lacy, too, Viola Bankes claimed that when she, a second daughter, was born in 1900 her mother wept and her father refused to see her. He even delayed registering her birth for several months. The situation was very different two years later when a son was born. There was rejoicing 'on a magnificent scale … Congratulations poured in, and festivities were arranged all over the estate.'

Those wives who failed to bear a child at all often felt this as a blot on their femininity and, as with Lady Frederick Cavendish, it could cause much anguish.

In the early and mid-Victorian years women, even in the 'best circles', often had large families, at a time when both maternal and infant mortality remained relatively high. Puerperal fever was a particular danger for mothers. Hence there were cases like that of Mary, wife of the 6th Earl Beauchamp of Madresfield, who died following childbirth in 1876, aged thirty-two. She had given birth to five children in eight years of married life. The 6th Earl's own mother had also died in childbirth, leaving behind five children. They had been placed in the care of a humourless servant-turned-governess, Eliza Marks, who seems to have made her young charges attend church seven times a day on Sundays and then required them to summarise the contents of the sermon. In other cases, as with Lady Boileau of Ketteringham Hall, who eventually bore nine children, frequent pregnancies undermined their health. For much of her married life Catherine Boileau was a semi-invalid. Only following the greater use of contraceptives in the second half of the nineteenth century, and especially from the 1890s, was there a decline in family size and a consequent fall in maternal deaths or chronic illness.

When a baby was born much of the responsibility for its care was given to the nursery staff, although the extent to which this happened depended on a mother's own inclinations. When the future Lady Cottesloe of Swanbourne in Buckinghamshire engaged a nurse for her two young children in 1900 she

Opposite:
A nursery scene with one little boy on a rocking horse. (The Robert Opie Collection)

Above:
Nurse Dawson holding baby John Phillimore after his christening in May 1908 at Shedfield House, Hampshire. (Hampshire Record Office)

Above right:
A nanny with her young charge. She was probably teaching him to read. (Hampshire Record Office)

emphasised to the successful candidate that she would 'expect to be head of nursery' herself and would administer any medication required. She must be informed immediately if the children were unwell, and she also stressed the need for the nurse to be patient with them 'even when they [were] annoying.' The nanny was to 'enter into their games & be bright & merry with them & really mother them & love them.' It is not known if the chosen candidate, Nurse Mayne, matched up to these expectations.

Lady Leconfield wrote almost daily to her children's nurse when she was away from the Petworth estate and received detailed accounts of their health and daily doings. When at home she joined in their games, took them for walks, and gave them lessons, to supplement those provided by the governess. If they were ill she helped to nurse them. Lady Carnarvon, too, although she had to spend much time away from her youngest children during the late 1830s and early 1840s, partly because of her husband's poor health and consequent need to travel to warmer climates, nevertheless maintained close contact with them through their devoted nurse, Mary Morton. Years later, when Mrs Morton died in April 1869, the 4th Earl of Carnarvon, once one of her charges, wrote sadly to his mother: 'I feel the snapping of the unbroken chain of so many years of recollections of her.'

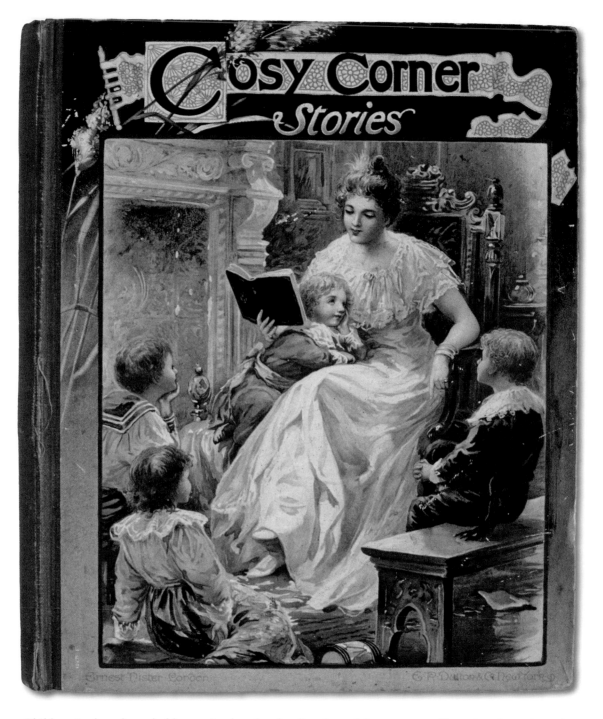

Children in these households remained under the direction of the nursery staff until they were five or six years of age. Indeed, up to the age of about four it was common to dress even the little boys in simple frocks, before they assumed more appropriate male attire. They then began lessons with a governess in the schoolroom. However, in their earliest years nurses not only looked after the youngsters' physical

A mother reading to her children. (The Robert Opie Collection)

welfare but taught them good personal habits and manners. Often, as with Mary Morton, they became part of their young charges' emotional life, particularly where parents were distant or neglectful, or where they followed a busy social round. Nannies might be left in sole charge of the children for long periods while their parents were away from home, or they might take them on holidays to the seaside

Sometimes a nanny was closer to the children than were their parents, especially if there were marital problems. Mrs Trotter was nurse to the children of John Edward Courtenay Bodley in the early 1900s. She remained with them when their parents divorced.

during the summer, when their parents were residing elsewhere. Winston Churchill, with an unaffectionate father and a socialite mother, relied very much on his nurse, Mrs Everest. She was his 'dearest and most intimate friend' for the first twenty years of his life, teaching him to read, taking him to pantomimes, and giving him unquestioning love and support. He was fond of his mother, Lady Randolph Churchill, too, but she seemed like 'a fairy princess'. She shone for him 'like the evening star. I loved her dearly – but at a distance.' Nonetheless she was interested in him in a way that her husband was not.

Nurses represented security and continuity in the lives of the children. But should they leave, this often caused deep distress. 'Without that familiar, all pervading presence,' recalled Lady Cynthia Asquith, 'I felt as if my whole known world were dissolving around me.' The substitution of a governess for a much-loved nurse could also prejudice the children against the newcomer. As Jessica Gerard points out, unlike schoolchildren, those taught by a governess could not escape her presence. 'Being naughty in lessons always led to reprisals in the rest of your life,' Viola Bankes lamented; 'you could not leave your school self behind at the end of the day.'

Most nannies were kind to their charges, but there were a few sadistic exceptions. They included Nurse Stanley, who looked after the Bankes children for some time. According to Viola, she introduced a regime of deprivation. 'Her one aim was

A governess in a country house with her young pupils, a brother and sister (1885). (Mary Evans Picture Library)

Mother (summoned by defeated nurse). " OH, MAUDIE DARLING, HOW *CAN* YOU BE SO NAUGHTY? " *Maudie.* " *EASILY!* "

Tantrums in the nursery (Punch, 1912).

apparently to make us miserable.' The widowed Mrs Bankes seemed not to notice what was happening until the serious illness of her beloved son led her to call in a London specialist. He discovered the children were not being fed properly and Nurse Stanley was at once dismissed. She was followed by efficient, brisk Nurse Startin and then by a succession of other nannies, who tended to pamper and spoil 'the little squire'.

To small children the large mansion in which they lived, lit only by candles, oil lamps or gas, could easily seem intimidating, especially during the dark winter months. At Stanway, the young Cynthia Charteris found the downstairs rooms 'vast, and for a long time uncharted regions'. Most of the children's time would be spent in the nursery, which was usually located on an upper floor or in a separate wing, away from adult members of the family. But as they grew older, many of them enjoyed visiting the servants' quarters 'below stairs'. Cynthia recalled how she relished being allowed by the cook to whisk an egg, or flatten dough with a rolling pin, or toss a pancake. She enjoyed, too, going into the butler's pantry where the footmen were busy setting trays or cleaning the silver, but 'were yet always ready to leave off to show us a card-trick or answer any number of riddles, and quite often generous enough to open a gushing bottle of ginger-beer or fizzy lemonade for our benefit.' At Kingston Lacy, too, when Mrs Bankes was away from home the children were able to play with the servants. The solidly dependable butler,

Mr Cooper not only doled out their pocket money but joined in games of cards or billiards. There was croquet and cricket, too. According to Viola Bankes, 'we easily made up an eleven with the staff from the kitchen, the pantry, the garage and the coach house.' In the summer they moved to a house the family owned at Studland Bay, a few miles away, where they played tennis, practised archery and bathed. They were also able to fish and ride, being taught the latter skill by the coachman, Crook.

Consuelo Marlborough, however, found the numerous servants got in the way of her desire to spend as much time as she could with her two small sons. As she later wrote ruefully: 'between the governess, the head nurse, and the groom with whom they rode their ponies, there seemed little time for mother.' She did, however, concede that the autocratic head nurse, despite a 'strange hostility to … youthful pleasures', nonetheless welcomed Consuelo's 'frequent visits to the nursery': 'I felt welcomed to those lovely hours I spent romping with my babies.'

The lives of most of the children were governed by a highly regulated daily routine designed to inculcate self-discipline and orderly behaviour. Sarah Sedgwick, who became a nursery maid at a large country house near Doncaster when she was fourteen, claimed that everything was governed by the clock. In this nursery there were two small children only, who were looked after by a head nurse, an under nurse, the nursery maid – Sarah herself – and a maid to wait on the nursery. In winter a footman came up every two hours to make up the fires. According to

Two small boys learning to play croquet at Sulham House, Berkshire, c. 1895. (Museum of English Rural Life, University of Reading)

Sarah, at 10 o'clock each morning they had to be out with the prams, which they pushed until half past twelve:

> Luncheon was one o'clock. Then from two until half past three another walk with the prams. This was followed by tea at four o'clock. Then there was dressing up the children before they went downstairs, and they were taken into the drawing-room to the minute, [to be with their parents] and brought up again to the minute. Then there were their baths to get ready … Then bed … Looking back on those days I think what a lot of dressing up children put up with, and what a lot of clothes they wore.

She stressed also their separation from the rest of the household. 'The nurseries were quite independent of the rest of the house, we had our own china, silver and linen.'

Nursery meals were plain and monotonous, and were prepared specially for the children. Even in affluent households the youngsters were often dressed in simple clothes and, as with Frances Maynard, the future Countess of Warwick, they might even wear hand-me-down garments. Toys were usually plentiful and, according to Lady Tweedsmuir, the shared games played on a shabby carpet of an ink-stained table cloth 'cemented solidarity between brothers and sisters'. Large gardens enabled the youngsters to play in safety, and many owned pets. They usually learned to ride at an early age.

Children were expected to be seen and not heard (Punch, 1896).

A FILIAL REPROOF.

Mamma (to Noel, who is inclined to be talkative). "HUSH NOEL! HAVEN'T I TOLD YOU OFTEN THAT LITTLE BOYS SHOULD BE *SEEN* AND NOT *HEARD?*"
Noel. "YES, MAMMA! BUT YOU DON'T *LOOK* AT ME!"

Frances Maynard had her first pony when she was five and could scarcely recollect a time when she could not ride. Dysart House on the Firth of Forth was the Scottish home of her stepfather, the Earl of Rosslyn. Although the house itself was ugly, this was more than compensated for by its beautiful grounds and the private bay where the children could 'bathe and swim and play during the long summer days'. Lady Rosslyn also ensured that the children received early lessons in their charitable duties. According to Millicent, another of her daughters, every afternoon they walked to the village carrying straw baskets containing the remnants of their luncheon. These were then distributed among the cottagers. 'Millicent hated the custom; she had already begun to develop an awareness of social injustice.' That feeling she was able to give effect to later in life when she married and became the Duchess of Sutherland. As the wife of an immensely rich landowner she initiated a number of charitable and self-help ventures on and around her husband's extensive estates in Scotland and Staffordshire.

Mothers and older sisters sometimes gave lessons to the younger children, as Lady Leconfield did. But governesses were recruited, too, perhaps to free a mother for other activities or because they offered expertise unavailable within the family. Instruction was given in a domestic setting and in the case of the girls rarely extended beyond 'accomplishments', such as foreign languages, music, drawing and dancing, as well as the 'basics' of reading, writing, simple arithmetic, and religious subjects. Those girls who wanted to pursue a more academic programme were discouraged, as it was thought that the label of 'blue-stocking' would harm their subsequent chances of making an advantageous match. For, as Lady Greville reminded mothers and

Alice Bonham Carter in the schoolroom at Ditcham Grove, Hampshire, in 1837. (Hampshire Record Office)

Children's games: playing 'Oranges and Lemons' at a Victorian children's party, c. 1850. (Mary Evans Picture Library)

daughters, marriage was 'the chief end and object of the Gentlewoman in Society … The existence of an aristocratic spinster, … turned out in middle age to endure grinding poverty and wearisome idleness, is … most pitiable.'

Nevertheless girls like Cynthia Charteris and Constance de Rothschild regretted the lack of practical teaching they received. According to Constance, her governess at Aston Clinton gave no lessons in cookery or dressmaking, and she and her sister

THE CHILD OF THE PERIOD.

Visitor at Country House. "BY THE BYE, YOU DIDN'T KNOW WHO I WAS THIS MORNING, MARGUERITE!"
Small Daughter of the House. "NO; WHO WERE YOU?"

A child of the period! Punch in 1885 drew rather disapproving attention to a precocious little girl.

A tactless young niece bringing a length of artificial hair as well as gloves to her aunt. In the background other children were playing croquet (Punch, 1867).

WHAT A MISTAKE!

Aunt. "HAVE YOU BROUGHT MY GLOVES, POLLY?"
Polly. "YES, AUNTY, AND YOUR LONG CURL, TOO, WHICH WAS LYING ON THE TABLE."

were 'not taught to dispense with the services of a maid'. She could remember 'very few historical dates and was also a very indifferent arithmetician'. But she was well schooled in English, French and German, and was encouraged to recite poetry and to write. Deportment, too, played a distinct part in the curriculum. As Angela, the Earl of Rosslyn's youngest child, noted ruefully, they received lessons 'stretched on a backboard, or sitting with straps and what-nots on our shoulders and our feet in stocks.' They were also taught the importance of social solidarity and appropriate conduct. Hence when eight-year-old Blanche Balfour at Inveraray argued with her aunt outside the door of the church, she was firmly reproved, being told she had

Boys at Eton College outside the tuck shop in the early 1900s. From the mid-nineteenth century increasing numbers of the sons of landed families attended a public school.

An idealised picture of children reading a fairy story quietly in the garden, c. 1880. (Mary Evans Picture Library)

broken 'the law about dignity and reticence in the presence of a different class'. Years later she still remembered the reprimand.

Boys might be instructed by a governess in their early years before they were handed over to tutors, but increasingly they were sent away to school while still young or they would spend time in the household of a clergyman who would give them lessons. By the middle of the nineteenth century attendance at a public school was becoming common among older boys. That was the case with Lord Porchester, heir to the Earl of Carnarvon. By his own wish he went to Eton in the spring of

1844, together with a cousin. But his father was anxious that he should receive suitable moral training, and insisted that he be accompanied by a private tutor as well. This was done despite the opposition of his Eton tutor. After the 3rd Earl's premature death in 1849, his widow determined to guide the morals of her offspring, including her second son, Alan, when he, too, went away to school. She was particularly concerned about his sporting activities and the influence being exerted in this regard by a fellow pupil. 'Enjoy your Gun, & your Cricket & Bathing, & whatever else may be going on, but let these be your relaxations, and do not let them upon *any pretence* interfere with your duties.' As regards pursuits like ratting, 'there is always something very degrading to the mind when *Man* the master spirit *looks on* applauding & encouraging two *lower* animals to tear each other to pieces. This is the reason that Cock fighting, Ferretting – Ratting, Dog fights &c. &c. are all odious, ungentlemanlike, barbarous and corrupting.' As she reminded him, '*You* … have been so differently brought up in this respect that there can be no danger of your being led into it.' Later in the same year, 1853, she reminded him that if he had any spare cash, it should be put 'into the poor box, this being a hard year with all the poor People'.

After public school, most of the young men went up to Oxford or Cambridge universities. Lord Willoughby de Broke of Compton Verney was one young aristocrat who followed this traditional path. After Eton, he entered New College, Oxford, in 1888. There he found the relaxed life of an undergraduate a welcome contrast to the school regime. Friendships were forged which would last a lifetime,

'A college wine' at Oxford University. Growing numbers of young men from landed families attended university during the second half of the nineteenth century. There they devoted themselves to pleasure rather than serious academic studies, as the illustration suggests. (Images and Voices, Oxfordshire County Council)

"A College Wine," Oxford.

and academic work imposed a comparatively light burden on all but the most ambitious or scholarly. During the winter there were plenty of opportunities for fox hunting, a particular passion with Willoughby de Broke, and there was cricket in summer. He emerged from New College with 'an easy degree, cricket, hunting and [skill in] driving four horses; the last three being very necessary accomplishments to the life that seemed to be indicated for me'.

Attendance at a public school, followed by a spell at university, also helped in the assimilation process for the sons of the nouveaux riches, though that process was not always easy. When John Stewart Parnell went up to Magdalene College, Cambridge in 1865, he observed snobbishly that the sons of wealthy parvenus 'from the North of England tried to liken themselves to country gentlemen and succeeded in looking like stable boys'. But many did make the transition. They included the son of Sir Francis Crossley. The Crossleys were members of the Halifax carpet-making firm and in the early 1860s Sir Francis acquired Somerleyton Hall in Suffolk as his country seat. His son, the second baronet, was educated at Eton and Balliol College, Oxford, before eventually he became Baron Somerleyton. By that time he had severed all connection with 'trade' and enjoyed instead the lifestyle and income of a rentier.

*Court gowns worn at the Drawing Room held by Queen Victoria at Buckingham Palace in May 1897, the year of her Diamond Jubilee (*The Queen, *22 May 1897).*

Although new girls' schools catering for the well-to-do had been set up by the mid-Victorian years, they were rarely attended by the daughters of landed families. As one peeress pronounced magisterially: '*We* do not send our daughters away to school.' However, when they reached the age of sixteen or seventeen, and before they formally 'came out' into adult society, some of them spent a year or so at a French, Swiss or German finishing school. This offered the usual range of 'accomplishments', with fluency in French considered a particularly desirable female attribute. Blanche Balfour, granddaughter of the 8th Duke of Argyll, went for the winter of 1896–7 to Dresden with a friend of her own age and a governess. 'Dresden', she wrote, 'was a great place for "finishing" education, and the town was full of English girls we knew.' As part of the process they made regular visits to the opera.

After her return, in the spring of 1898 Blanche was duly presented at court at one of the Queen's official Drawing Rooms. It was a sign that she had left the

A debutante presented to King Edward VII and Queen Alexandra at a Drawing Room held in 1903.

schoolroom behind her, and could put up her hair, lengthen her skirts, acquire a fashionable wardrobe, and participate in the pleasures of the London Season, which ran from April or May to the end of July in each year. Without being presented, declared *Etiquette for Ladies* (1900), 'a girl has no recognised position … prior to this … she is a "juvenile", but after making her profound curtsey to Royalty she leaves the magic presence a "grown up"!' During the last twenty years of Queen Victoria's reign, the number of presentations more than doubled. This necessitated the addition of a fourth Drawing Room in 1880, to supplement the existing three, and a fifth in 1895. Usually a mother would present her daughter or, if the mother were dead, the role would be taken by another relative or older married friend.

Many debutantes found presentation an ordeal, fearing to commit a *faux pas* which would disgrace them before their elders and their peers. Hence the nervousness of Constance Weld early in May 1874 when she and her sister Agnes came up from their quiet Dorset home to London for a Drawing Room. Their mother was dead, so the sponsoring role was taken by a family friend. Constance wrote,

> The long dreaded Presentation day … arrived at last … our dresses came very late and fitted atrociously – I never suffered such a fearful day in my whole life – Charlotte Horningold presented us, we started from her home at ½ twelve & didn't get to Buckingham Palace until after three. The Presentation was a very different thing to what I had thought – I did all sorts of wrong things – seized hold of the Queen's hand for one thing … When we had left the royal presence came the most fearful part of the day – down at the entrance the pushing, shoving & want of order altogether was dreadful – we didn't get away until 6.30 … quite tired & exhausted we both were.

A LAMENT.

Dowager. "It's been the worst Season I can remember, Sir James! All the Men seem to have got Married, and none of the Girls!"

Some younger women, like Lord Suffield's daughter Cecilia, carried out a programme of self-improvement while joining in the wider social events of the London Season. 'Alice and I have joined a reading society', Cecilia noted in her diary, Alice being a younger sister. The following month she, another sister and their German governess-cum-chaperon went 'to see the Old Masters at the Royal Academy'. After this came 'A Ball at Dudley House to which we all went. One of the prettiest & best balls I have ever been to. A great many new young ladies were there.'

As they went about, the debutantes were carefully chaperoned, and some mothers placed special restrictions on their daughters' activities. Ishbel Marjoribanks's mother, for example, had a rule that her daughter should not attend more than three dances a week during the Season, 'unless under exceptional circumstances … Her strict injunction was never to dance more than two dances with the same man, but I might go to tea or supper with him in addition, if I so desired.'

All the girls were aware that a major role of the Season was to serve as a marriage mart, with care taken to ensure that they met only the 'right' people, so that if and when they married, the spouse would be acceptable in all respects. For mothers it was a time of anxiety, as they devoted energy to this subtle form of social control. According to Victoria Glendinning, most ladies 'did not feel they were wasting their time paying morning calls, giving "At Homes", chaperoning their daughters at balls, working out who should go down to dinner with whom … This was their work, and their duty.' The rituals concerning such matters as the making of formal calls, the leaving of visiting cards, the securing of introductions, and the question of precedence on social occasions such as dinner parties were all matters of etiquette in which debutantes had to be schooled. After her marriage, Consuelo Marlborough confessed to spending hours ensuring that the rules of precedence were carefully observed for guests at dinner parties. That applied not merely to seating arrangements but to the procession in to dinner.

A fortunate few debutantes made a suitable match in their first Season. They included Frances Maynard, who as an heiress in her own right with an annual income of £40,000, was a 'catch' for any potential husband. In her case a proposal was accepted from Lord Brooke, heir to the 5th Earl of Warwick. But a number of

THE TROUSSEAU

PAINTED BY HARRISON FISHER

© REINTHAL & NEWMAN, PUBS., N. Y.

The selection of a trousseau was an important part of the marriage preparations.

girls had to experience several Seasons before an eligible suitor appeared. According to Jessica Gerard, the average age at marriage for heirs' wives was twenty-four, which, as she points out, was probably seven or eight years after they came out.

At a time when falling rentals in the final quarter of the nineteenth century, coupled with a lavish lifestyle, put pressure on the finances of many landed families, girls without a substantial dowry found difficulty in making a good match. That situation was aggravated by the entry of the daughters of the nouveaux riches into High Society, and also by the growing number of marriages between aristocrats and the daughters of wealthy American businessmen. The arrival of the latter caused resentful English mothers to complain of the predatory instincts of the transatlantic interlopers, fearing the effect of the competition on their own daughters' marital prospects. Lady Dorothy Nevill noted that it was in the 1870s that the spate of Anglo-American marriages began, with Jennie Jerome and Lord Randolph Churchill among the pioneers. But, as Lady Dorothy drily conceded, there were 'many old families which, both in mind and pocket, have been completely revivified

A French fashion plate of the early 1850s, when crinolines were in vogue. The suppliers of the clothes were detailed for the benefit of future purchasers.

LES MODES PARISIENNES

by … marriages with American brides'. The marriage between the 8th Duke of Marlborough and the wealthy American widow Lilian Hammersley in the late 1880s enabled electric lighting, more bathrooms and an improved system of central heating to be installed at Blenheim Palace, for example.

In all, between 1870 and 1914 there were at least 102 American women who married peers or the sons of peers and by the early 1900s they were accounting for nearly one in ten of all peers' marriages. Among those arranged in the mid-1890s were those between Consuelo Vanderbilt and the 9th Duke of Marlborough and between Mary Leiter, whose father had made a fortune in Chicago real estate, and George Curzon, eldest son and heir of Viscount Scarsdale of Kedleston Hall, Derbyshire. It was Mr Leiter's cash that paid for much of his son-in-law's political campaigning, and enabled him three years after marriage financially to support his position as Viceroy of India. But Mary was aware that her union with the eligible eldest son of Lord Scarsdale had been greeted with hostility. 'My path is strewn with roses, and the only thorns are the unforgiving women', she wrote to her parents soon after the wedding.

Often the dowry of an American bride enabled her husband to refurbish his property. This was true of the 8th Duke of Roxburghe, who in 1903 married May Goelet. She was the daughter of Ogden Goelet, who had himself inherited a fortune in New York real estate. May's marriage settlement was estimated by the press to be in the region of £2 million, a truly vast sum at that date. Floors Castle in Kelso, the Duke's family seat, was completely transformed by the young Duchess, with much gilding, panelling and pale pink brocade upholstery in the main salon, as well as the display of valuable tapestries.

Left:
Lady Randolph Churchill, the former Miss Jennie Jerome, was one of the first American brides to marry into the British aristocracy.

Few English-born brides would have been able to command such large sums as many of these young American 'invaders'. Hence the angry comment by Marie Corelli, a popular contemporary novelist: 'America's … influence on the social world [has taught] that "dollars are the only wear". English Society has been sadly vulgarized by this American taint.' The criticism conveniently ignored the fact that for centuries marriages among the landed classes had normally been preceded by lengthy negotiations over cash settlements and dowries and this had been accepted as part of the expected ritual.

Below:
The bicycling craze in the late nineteenth century seems to have beguiled a mother and son at Sulham House in Berkshire. (Museum of English Rural Life, University of Reading)

Chapter Four

OUT OF DOORS

IMPORTANT FEATURES of any country house were the extensive grounds that surrounded it, and the leisure activities associated with them. As Phyllida Barstow has written, sport was the foundation on which country-house parties were based. 'The winter sports usually involved killing something and the summer ones hitting a ball.'

Also significant was the estate yard itself, with its range of workshops employing craftsmen and maintenance staff, including carpenters, painters, masons, blacksmiths, and in a few cases electricians. There were also stable workers, as well as farm labourers and a bailiff employed on the home farm, plus a large number of gardeners and gamekeepers. These last were involved in embellishing the estate and striving to provide many of the pleasures and pastimes associated with it. In total it could represent a very large-scale enterprise indeed. At Eaton, the Duke of Westminster's staff of over three hundred men and women included a head gardener with forty underlings, seventy men who worked under the head forester, and forty on the home farm under a bailiff. The Duke also owned racehorses, including two winners of the Derby, and he placed great reliance on the judgement of Richard Chapman, his stud groom from 1880. Chapman had thirty men and boys working for him.

It is perhaps not surprising, therefore, that when Sir Robert Peel visited Woburn Abbey in 1849 he was struck by the size and complexity of the estate yard, describing it as 'more like a dockyard than a domestic office'. Lady Gregory, who grew up at Roxborough in Ireland, similarly referred to the 'life and stir' that characterised a major working estate. Roxborough formed a 'complete community within itself … The estate had its own smithy, sawmill, and carpenters' workshops; its coach-houses, cow-houses, dairy, laundry, piggery, kennels … The yard at Roxborough was a microcosm of the outside world.' This was reflected in the experience of many country-house families elsewhere.

Friendships, too, were often formed between senior members of the outdoor staff and their employers in a way that rarely applied to their indoor counterparts. That was especially true of head gardeners and gamekeepers. At Chatsworth the 6th Duke of Devonshire not only encouraged the innovative skills of his head gardener, Joseph Paxton, while he created one of the country's most famous gardens, but in 1849 he appointed Paxton agent for the whole estate, with the substantial salary of £500 a year. He held the post until the Duke's death in 1858. He also accompanied his employer on tours to inspect some of the leading gardens in Europe, and when the Duke died he bequeathed £2,000 to Paxton in his will. More modestly, three of the Duke's senior gamekeepers were left the equivalent of a year's wages.

Lord Willoughby de Broke enjoyed close ties with Jesse Eales, the long-serving head keeper on the Compton Verney estate. Years later he called the gamekeeper his 'first and … best friend', after his parents, and described how Eales had introduced

Opposite:
Lord Granard taking aim at a pheasant at a shooting party at Warter Priory, home of the Wilsons. His American-born wife seemed not to appreciate the noise of the guns (The Tatler, *January 1911).*

Gardeners at work at Purley Hall in 1864, with some genteel female onlookers in the background. (Museum of English Rural Life, University of Reading)

Below: A shooting party at Whomerly Wood, Stevenage, in 1894, showing the quantity of game killed as well as the beaters (some of whom were very young) and the sportsmen themselves. (Museum of English Rural Life, University of Reading)

Right:
Lord Willoughby de Broke of Compton Verney, an enthusiastic Master
of the Warwickshire Hounds and a keen follower of hunting in general.

Below:
An example of skilled topiary at Levens Hall, Westmorland (now
Cumbria) in 1911 – an indication of the creative abilities of the
gardeners. (Mary Evans Picture Library)

him to a wide range of field sports. 'It was with him I saw my first fox killed; it was with him that I killed my first pheasant, partridge, duck, hare, rabbit and rook; also my first fish.' Fox-hunting was to become the great passion of Willoughby de Broke's life. For many years he was Master of the Warwickshire Hounds and he subsequently claimed that hunting 'four times a week for seven months in the year [was] not a profession that [afforded] much leisure for entertaining'. It was also expensive. The 5th Earl Spencer, another hunting enthusiast, had two spells as Master of the Pytchley Hounds in the 1860s and 1870s, and was then obliged in April 1879 to seek a loan for £15,000 'on account of the excess expenditure for the Hounds, 1874–78'.

Right:
An unskilful sportsman tempted to commit the unpardonable sin, in the eyes of country gentlemen, of shooting a fox (Punch, 1889). The frequency with which Punch *featured sporting cartoons indicates their popularity with its readers.*

"EVERY EXCUSE."

Brigson (excited). "HULLO!—THERE GOES A—"
His Host (clutching his arm). "GOOD HEAVENS!—YOU'RE NOT GOING TO SHOOT THAT FOX?"
Brigson. "MY DEAR F'LLER! WH'-WH'-WHY NOT? THIS IS THE LAST DAY I SHALL HAVE THIS SEASON—AND I—I FEEL AS IF I COULD SHOOT MY OWN MOTHER-IN-LAW—IF SHE ROSE!"

[Ups with his gun!

Below:
Preparations for a beagle hunt at the beginning of the 1900s. (Museum of English Rural Life, University of Reading)

The estate craftsmen carried out repairs to the cottages and other buildings as well as working on the mansion itself, while the main tasks of the blacksmiths were shoeing the horses and making or repairing metal gates and some of the tools in use on the property. By the late 1880s and the 1890s some estates, like Blenheim, were recruiting electricians, who enjoyed additional prestige as modern technicians, being treated with the respect due to 'men of science'.

The stable staff looked after the horses and the carriages, with the head groom expected to provide his employer with up-to-date details concerning the health and welfare of the animals. Henry Palmer, the head groom at Althorp, wrote frequent and detailed accounts of the condition of the horses under his charge to Earl Spencer, as well as mentioning the deficiencies of individual stable workers. Later, as motor vehicles increased in number, stable staff were reduced and some coachmen trained to become chauffeurs. Often they received instruction at the factories where the cars were built, since they would be expected to carry out repairs as well as drive the vehicles.

Among the most important of the outdoor workers were the gardeners. They cultivated the pleasure grounds, the flower gardens, and the kitchen garden with its multiplicity of hothouses. At Trentham, for example, about a third of the 5-acre kitchen garden was said to be under glass. The hothouses were used to raise exotic

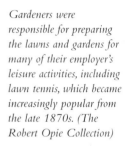

Gardeners were responsible for preparing the lawns and gardens for many of their employer's leisure activities, including lawn tennis, which became increasingly popular from the late 1870s. (The Robert Opie Collection)

Members of the Curtis family at Alton, Hampshire, taking tea in their garden in the mid-1860s. (Hampshire Museums Service)

fruit and flowers, such as orchids, as well as out-of-season vegetables. According to Robert Fish, writing in 1857, it was 'the first duty of a gardener … to provide his employer's table with plenty of good flavoured vegetables'. Some gardeners were also skilled decorators, arranging elaborate floral displays in the house itself.

The kitchen garden was especially significant because on the quality of its produce often depended an owner's reputation for hospitality. Some cooks would summarily reject anything they considered sub-standard. At Knowsley, seat of the Earl of Derby, thirty-nine gardeners were employed early in the twentieth century, tending the flower borders, weeding and caring for the lawns, and cultivating an enormous kitchen garden, whose produce was consumed either at Knowsley itself or at Stanley House at Newmarket. For the latter purpose it had to be carefully packed in hampers for onward despatch by rail. Derby House in London was supplied from Coworth Park, a country estate near Sunningdale, which the Earl had acquired in 1895.

Ernest Field, who worked for Alfred de Rothschild as a journeyman-propagator on his Halton estate in Buckinghamshire, recalled his employer as a man who expected an immediate response to his orders. One summer, after a long dry spell had burned all the lawns brown, he apparently threatened to have them painted green. 'Fortunately the weather changed just in time', recalled Field drily. Staff at Halton, as on many other estates with strong-minded owners, took care to follow the advice of the Longleat head gardener William Taylor when he declared that whatever the provocation, it was essential to maintain self control in the presence of an employer.

At the end of the nineteenth century the Halton garden staff numbered about sixty, and among their tasks was caring for fifty glasshouses filled with choice plants. 'I once heard it said', noted Ernest Field, 'that rich people used to show their wealth by the size of their bedding-plant list: 10,000 plants for a squire; 20,000 for a baronet; 30,000 for an earl and 50,000 for a duke. Mr Rothschild aimed pretty high, because my list for 1903, with no fewer than 40,418 plants, put him well above an earldom.' It was the skill and hard work of the Halton gardeners that enabled Alfred de Rothschild to display his largesse by sending guests away with huge boxes of hothouse flowers and great baskets of exotic fruit.

Like many other stately home gardeners, Field spent some of his spare time in visiting other estates, to make contact with their staff and to compare the quality of their work with his own.

While most owners relied on their head gardener or a landscape specialist to redesign their grounds from time to time, some preferred to take an active role themselves. Among them was Mary Anne Disraeli. When rebuilding work was under way at Hughenden in the 1860s she decided to change the garden, too. Although she was in her seventies, she spent many hours out of doors supervising the work, clad for the purpose in a short skirt and gaiters. A packed lunch and bottles of beer were supplied to the workers, and in the end she felt great satisfaction at the effect she had created. As she told the young Lord Rosebery, when her husband returned

A genteel picnic in the grounds of a country house featured in this advertisement for Huntley & Palmers biscuits. (The Robert Opie Collection)

THE PICNIC, (EPPING FOREST.)

to Hughenden and said, '"this is quite delightful, better than anything you have done yet", … I feel quite intoxicated for the moment, and quite rewarded.'

The Bedfordshire squire John Brooks of Flitwick was another keen gardener. In pursuit of his hobby he attended horticultural shows in London as well as visiting the gardens of other gentlemen as often as he could. He also maintained a correspondence with some of the leading head gardeners in the locality. Among them was the Duke of Bedford's gardener, Forbes, at Woburn Abbey. Brooks purchased seeds and plants from nurserymen up and down the country, and when he entertained he prided himself on the wide range of dessert fruit he could offer which had been grown on the estate. In August 1848, for example, he noted that at a dinner for friends and neighbours he had been able to provide twenty dishes of dessert, including grapes, apricots, strawberries, pears, currants, and much more besides. However, he apparently did not raise pineapples and melons, which were expensive to grow and were the prestige fruit favoured by the aristocracy.

Those country house owners who were unable to enjoy a wide range of high-quality home-grown garden produce blamed their head gardener for the deficiency. In June 1870 the Gloucestershire squire Dearman Birchall wrote gloomily: 'I want a gardener. Bevan is not a manager with other servants I fear. We seem the only people with no strawberries or cherries, or nice salad or young potatoes.' Not until August 1873 did he finally recruit William Keen as head gardener on his Bowden estate, at a salary of £80 a year. Keen remained there for about fifty years.

Four ladies playing croquet at Sulham House, c. 1894. The preparation of a croquet lawn was another requirement for many country-house gardeners. (Museum of English Rural Life, University of Reading)

To demonstrate their professional skills and perhaps to impress potential and actual employers, ambitious country-house gardeners competed for prizes at horticultural shows. At Kingston Lacy Viola Bankes remembered that Mr Hill, the Scottish-born head gardener, would not allow peaches or grapes to be picked that he was raising for the local horticultural show. 'With ten gardeners in winter and twenty in summer, some of whom worked only in the hot houses, it was no wonder that the local people began to object to my mother's flowers, fruit and vegetables continually carrying off the prizes.' Viola recalled that Hill was 'feared and hated' by the under-gardeners, and that he was 'always bad tempered on Saturdays, when he was irritated at having to part with some of his precious flowers for church decoration.'

Gardeners began their career as boy apprentices under a head gardener, who usually proved a strict taskmaster. Scottish head gardeners were favoured by English estate owners because they were thought to be better trained than their English or Welsh counterparts. After serving a few years and learning the rudiments of his trade, the youngster progressed to become a journeyman, and later a foreman. Those who aimed high recognised that the best instruction would be provided in the gardens of the aristocracy, and some of the most successful – or avaricious – head gardeners charged their apprentices a fee. Others, like James Barnes of Bicton Park and Joseph Paxton at Chatsworth, imposed fines on their subordinates as a punishment for neglecting their duties or offending in other ways. At Bicton, anyone

Rinking (or skating) was very popular in the 1870s. It provided opportunities for discreet flirtations away from the censorious eye of a chaperon (Punch, 1876).

coming to work on a Monday morning in a dirty shirt or arriving on any morning with shoes improperly laced, could be fined 3d. A similar penalty was incurred for taking a wheelbarrow with a dirty wheel on the walks or leaving a gate or door open in any part of the garden.

To gain promotion an apprentice usually had to move to a different estate, perhaps obtaining the post through an advertisement in *The Gardeners' Chronicle*, which was the leading trade newspaper, or by personal recommendation from his employer or his head gardener. As he moved around to gain experience and promotion, he, like other young unmarried gardeners, would usually reside in a bothy, which was a kind of lodging house provided by the employer. It was fitted out with bedding and a little furniture, while a cleaner and perhaps a cook would also be supplied. Produce from the garden usually formed part of the pay, but for the rest the youngsters had to cater for themselves. Working hours were long, especially when they were employed in the glasshouses, since it was essential to keep the temperature in these constant, to ensure that the plants were not damaged. Sixty hours a week was not an uncommon stint for junior staff. Once a man had risen to be an experienced foreman, his head gardener might try to obtain a head gardener's place for him. From the 1850s leading nurseries like James Veitch & Sons of Chelsea also acted as recruitment agencies on behalf of clients, as well as keeping a register of men and boys who were seeking new posts.

Gardeners were important to the country house not merely for the enjoyment they provided through the cultivation of colourful flower beds, the creation of pleasant walks, and the high quality fruit and vegetables they raised, but in other ways. It was their skill that created the carefully manicured lawns needed for summer sports like croquet, archery, cricket, and, in the 1870s and beyond, lawn tennis. Croquet parties were popular from the 1860s, as the diary of Lady Knightley of

A croquet contest at Luton Hoo in the early 1860s. Croquet owed something of its appeal to the fact that it could be played by both men and women. (Luton Museum and Art Gallery)

Fawsley confirms. She was a keen player and, unlike many other sports, it was a game in which both men and women could join. In August 1870 Lady Knightley noted that she and her husband had held their 'first big party for the neighbours' by issuing invitations to play croquet from 4 p.m. to 7 p.m. About a hundred people attended: 'we had a band & gave them refreshments in the Old Hall & it all went off very well.'

Garden parties were another way of entertaining 'the neighbours', and as Elinor Glyn, wife of a minor Essex squire, commented, they had the merit of being more 'inclusive' than invitations to lunch or dinner. Soon after Elinor's marriage a 'dowager, who was endeavouring to initiate me into my county duties, advised me with regard to invitations for the first garden party which I gave at Sheering Hall. "Remember, my dear," she said, … "it is only to garden parties that you must ask the lawyers and doctors – never to luncheons or dinners!"'.

Some country houses like Wilton or Easton Lodge, Lady Warwick's Essex home, held cricket weeks. 'We used to put up at least two teams in the house, spread a big luncheon tent, and invite the county to see the play', she wrote. Her elder son, Guy, was an enthusiastic player. On a wider basis the annual Eton and Harrow cricket match at Lord's and that between Oxford and Cambridge universities were regarded as integral parts of the London Season.

In the 1890s bicycling became popular and it was common for machines to be taken along to country-house parties. Girls particularly welcomed this as it enabled them to escape from the surveillance of their chaperons. Lady Angela Forbes, the

Punch drawing attention to the dilemma of an umpire at a ladies' doubles tennis match (1884).

LAWN TENNIS.
TRIALS OF THE UMPIRE AT A LADIES' DOUBLE.
Lilian and Claribel. "IT WAS OUT, WASN'T IT, CAPTAIN STANDISH?"
Adeline and Eleanore. "OH, IT WASN'T OUT, CAPTAIN STANDISH, WAS IT?"

Right:
A garden party with an archery contest in full swing (Punch, 1867).

Below:
The Vyne cricket team in Hampshire in August 1871. The Vyne was owned by the Chutes and surviving score books show that several family members played for the team in the 1870s. Their opponents included teams from other country houses in the county, such as Highclere and Breamore. (Hampshire Record Office)

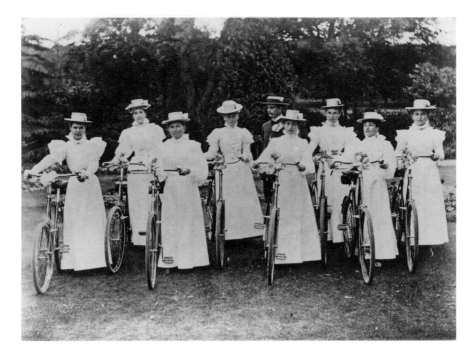

Countess of Warwick's half-sister, claimed that when the bicycling craze was at its height everyone 'had their bicycle painted a different colour; bicycle stables were built and bicycles became a part of everyone's luggage.' Some country house parties were arranged to coincide with the major race meetings at Newmarket, Ascot, Goodwood, Doncaster and Epsom. The Prince of Wales shared the commitment to horse racing and already in the 1860s Queen Victoria was urging him to reduce the number of race meetings he attended, but without success. According to Lady Warwick, he 'never missed Newmarket, and would frequently ride out with the rest of us in the mornings to see the horses exercised'. Later he acquired his own stable and in 1896 one of his horses won the Derby – a feat that he was to repeat with two other horses in 1900 and 1907.

The traditional country sports of hunting, shooting and fishing provided the main out-of-doors recreation, however, for landed families, and especially for the menfolk. In the second half of the nineteenth century, increasing numbers of women went hunting, too. They included Lady Angela Forbes and the Countess of Warwick. Lady Warwick hunted extensively not only in the shire counties of England but in Ireland, where she had some of her 'most

'exciting' runs with the Meath pack and the celebrated Ward Stag-hounds. 'I used to go over … specially for the hunting.' Not even serious falls and broken bones deterred her.

Earl Spencer of Althorp shared her enthusiasm, although his wife did not. On more than one occasion she had to make her own way to visit friends or to return home because he had been delayed at a meet. She seems to have accepted it with good grace, although on at least one occasion, when she and her husband were to stay at Belvoir Castle, it must have been embarrassing. They had been invited so that Lord Spencer could hunt with the Belvoir pack, but he failed to meet his wife at Northampton railway station, as they had arranged, because he had gone out with the Pytchley. She made her own way to Belvoir, where she was greeted by the Duke and Duchess of Rutland. On arrival she was shown straight to her room and in the evening they first sat 'in a small drawing-room downstairs', before the party went upstairs to the ballroom. There the 'Duke's militia band played & we danced'. Spencer himself finally arrived at 11 p.m. and had to pass through the ballroom in his muddy hunting gear on the way to his own room. Apparently he 'had had a good run & missed two trains – hence his late arrival'.

The Earl's other interests included rifle shooting, deer stalking and game shooting. On occasion these latter involved lengthy visits to Scotland, where Charlotte Spencer, like most other ladies at these shooting parties, amused herself as best she could by gossiping, walking and visiting local beauty spots, while awaiting the return of the menfolk in the evening after their day's sport. Lady Wortley was not alone in

The Meet, *painted by Heywood Hardy (1842– 1933). (Christie's Images / The Bridgeman Art Library)*

IN THE HIGHLANDS.

A Highland scene showing a party of sportsmen, perhaps engaged in deer stalking as well as the consumption of Huntley & Palmers biscuits! (The Robert Opie Collection)

complaining of the many hours of boredom that resulted: 'I sometimes feel that for part of the year I am married to a gun, not a man.'

Lady Warwick, too, found fishing and shooting parties uninteresting. As she later wrote, her husband was

> such a crack shot that we were asked everywhere, Blenheim, Chatsworth, and all the great places. The average party might number sixteen … We began the day by breakfasting at ten o'clock. This meal consisted of many courses … The men went out shooting after breakfast and then came the emptiness of the long morning from which I suffered silently. I can remember the groups of women sitting discussing their neighbours or writing letters at impossible little ornamental tables … The 'ladies' … rarely took part in the shoot, not even going out to join the shooters until luncheon time. Then, dressed in tweeds …, we went out together to some rendezvous of the shooters. A woman who was very bloodthirsty and sporting might go and cower behind some man and watch his prowess among the pheasants. But there were very few … After a large luncheon, finishing up with coffee and liqueurs, the women preferred to wend their way back to the house. They would spend the intervening time until the men returned for tea …, changing their clothes. This time they got into lovely tea-gowns … We changed our clothes four times a day at least. This kept our maids and ourselves extraordinarily busy … Conversation at tea was slumberous. Nobody woke up to be witty until dinner time with its accompanying good wines. The men discussed the bags of the day and the

women did the admiring … It used often to be sheer boredom until seven when we went off to dress for dinner … [A]fter some experience of such parties I used to try to get out of invitations and let my husband go alone.

Nevertheless, Lady Warwick's dislike of shooting parties did not prevent her from holding them at Easton Lodge, where the guests were able to combine sporting activities with discreet flirtation – this last being something at which the hostess herself was very adept.

Game shooting and, to a lesser extent, deer stalking in Scotland became popular country-house sports in the second half of the nineteenth century. They also became increasingly plutocratic because of the high cost of raising and protecting the game, which meant employing large numbers of keepers and other workers to rear and protect the birds and animals concerned. The sport appealed to the nouveaux riches as well as to established landed families because by holding a shoot it was possible for a parvenu to become part of High Society. The process was encouraged by the Prince of Wales's own keenness for the sport. Those who did not purchase shooting estates of their own could rent them from existing landowners, thereby boosting the latter's income at a time of agricultural depression. According to Phyllida Barstow, traditional owners like the Earls of Seafield and Breadalbane in Scotland found that 'millionaire tenants were eager to rent their outlying deer-forests for outrageous

A shooting luncheon at Easton Lodge, Essex, home of the Earl and Countess of Warwick in 1895. In the centre of the back row was the Prince of Wales, then a very close friend of Lady Warwick.

A SHOOTING LUNCHEON AT EASTON, OCTOBER, 1895

H.R.H. the Prince of Wales; Mrs. Ralph Sneyd; Lord De Lisle and Dudley; Blanche, Countess of Rosslyn; Mr. and Mrs. Menzies; Col. Mark Lockwood, M.P., and Mrs. Lockwood; Lady Lilian Wemyss; Lord Rosslyn; Lady Angela Forbes; Col. Sir Arthur Paget; Lord Herbert Vane Tempest; Miss Muriel Wilson; Mr. and Mrs. R. Woodhouse; Sir Walter Gilbey; Sir George Holford; Myself and my husband

sums. Five thousand pounds for ten weeks' sport was not unusual.' Stags were shot in the late summer and autumn, and the skill and patience needed to stalk them on the steep, barren hill-tops, under the guidance of experienced gillies, gave the sport its fascination. Deer ponies had to be trained to carry the dead stags, which could weigh as much as 20 stone.

Three developments in the Victorian era helped to promote the sport of shooting. The first was the technical improvement in the gun itself, which permitted more rapid and effective firing. The second was the building of the railway network, which made accessible moors which had hitherto been reached only with difficulty; and the final and most important change was the development of the battue system. By this the birds were driven by beaters over the guns, instead of the sportsman walking his estate with a pair of pointers and killing a few birds only. The hand rearing of pheasants, which occurred on an increasing scale during the second half of the nineteenth century, encouraged the process by providing the large bags which became a major feature of the sport. Owners competed with one another to provide the largest number of birds and it was the head keeper's responsibility to ensure that he and the under-keepers met that need. This involved the elimination of predators on a large scale as well as the preserving and nurturing of the birds themselves. The existence of stringent game laws meant that those found poaching could be brought before the courts and fined or imprisoned. But that did not prevent bitter and sometimes fatal skirmishes taking place between poachers and gamekeepers, especially in the first half of the nineteenth century.

At Elveden in Suffolk, one of the principal shooting estates, the property was purchased in 1894 by Lord Iveagh, whose fortune came from the Guinness brewing

Grouse shooting, probably in Scotland, in 1848, painted by Alexander Rolfe, fl. 1839–73. (Christie's Images / The Bridgeman Art Library)

A BAD SEASON.

Sportsman. "I can assure you, what with the Rent of the Moor, and my Expenses, and 'what not,' the Birds have cost me—ah—a Sovereign apiece!!"

Keeper. "A' weel, Sir! 'Deed it's a Maircy ye didna Kill na mair o' 'em!!"

Above:
Punch *ironically observing that high rentals for grouse moors did not always result in good 'bags' of birds (1867).*

Right:
*An advertisement offering to supply pheasants to boost estate game bags. 'Buying in' was one way of achieving this (*The Field, *3 October 1885).*

PHEASANTS and PARTRIDGES.—
Orders now BOOKED for the delivery of any number of Live PHEASANTS after Oct. 1, and PARTRIDGES after Sept. 1.—M. Robb, Esq., Game Farm, Liphook, Hants.

POULTRY.—During the ensuing week we shall have on Show the following: LIGHT and DARK BRAHMAS, Buff Cochins, Andalusians, Plymouth Rocks, Pile, Brown-red, and Black-breasted Game, Gold-pencilled and Black Hamburghs, Gold-spangled and Black White-crested Polands, Gold and Silver Sebrights Pigeons, &c.—C. Baker and Co., 20, Grand Avenue, Leaden hall Market.

PHEASANTS.—S. PUNTER, Pheasant Breeder and Licensed Game Dealer, begs respectfully to announce the REMOVAL of his PHEASANTRIES from Great Missenden to the Bank Farm, Wendover. Orders booked for any number of Poults at greatly reduced prices; satisfaction guaranteed.

PHEASANT - FEEDING RAISINS —
Reduced Price.—The superior quality, as supplied for many years to the nobility and gentry throughout the Kingdom, may still be obtained in 1cwt. bags at the reduced price of 16s., 5cwt. 15s.; delivered free to any London station.—P.O.O., to George Uphill, 33, St. Mary-at-Hill (late 33, Pudding-lane), London.

*Pheasant shooting.
'A good high bird' at
Studley Royal, Yorkshire,
one of the famous
shooting estates
(Country Life,
14 December 1901).
(Museum of English
Rural Life, University of
Reading)*

enterprise. During his first season 24,731 head of game were killed, 15,100 of them pheasants, 1,978 partridges, and 6,778 rabbits. The following year eggs were bought from game farms to supplement those raised on the estate itself. It was the task of the keepers to collect the estate pheasants' eggs from special laying fields, where the female birds were kept, and to place them under broody hens for hatching. The hens were purchased from local farmers. When they first emerged, the chicks had to be fed a special diet several times a day. The process was laborious but by the time the poults, as they had become, were about six to eight weeks old they were ready to be taken into the woods. There they were fed on a declining scale for a week or two more, before they were considered to have reverted to their wild state.

At Elveden as many as 20,000 pheasants were being reared annually by the end of the nineteenth century, with 108,392 head of game killed in the 1899–1900 season alone. Of these over 21,000 were pheasants and 83,319 were rabbits. By that date the game department at Elveden comprised seventy men, of whom twenty-four were liveried keepers and thirty were warreners.

On a national basis, too, the number of gamekeepers increased rapidly, although the growing preservation often created ill-feeling between the sportsmen and farmers in heavily preserved counties. The farmers complained of the crop damage caused by the game, and owners sometimes sought to placate them by distributing gifts of dead game after a shoot. Friends, too, might receive similar gifts.

The season began on the 'Glorious Twelfth' of August, when grouse shooting commenced. Men who were expert shots, like Lord Walsingham or Lord de Grey

AFTER THE BATTUE—AN AUTUMN IDYL.

Punch mocking the indiscriminate slaughter of game birds associated with the battue system of shooting (1881).

enjoyed considerable prestige among their peers, even though the incessant firing of the guns gave some of them severe headaches. The Duchess of Marlborough recalled that there was a record shoot one autumn at Blenheim when 7,000 rabbits were bagged by five expert marksmen. 'They had two loaders and three guns each, and every one of them had a violent headache on reaching home.'

The competitive urge and its associated mass slaughter of birds and animals was encouraged by the Prince of Wales himself. Over the years, from the 1860s, he spent about £300,000 in transforming the Sandringham estate into a world-famous shooting property, with a rise in the head of game shot each year from about 7,000 to 30,000. The spirit of rivalry was encouraged by the way in which an equerry would question each guest at the end of a drive as to how many birds he had shot. These figures were then read out over luncheon, to the satisfaction of the expert shots and the discomfiture of the less successful. Game books were kept and they meticulously recorded the daily cull, while reports of successful shoots appeared in the sporting press, such as *The Shooting Times* and *The Gamekeeper*.

Those landowners who invited the Prince of Wales to their shooting parties inevitably incurred much expense. In certain wealthy families it was the practice to refurbish the royal suite specially for each visit, while the chef who served for 'ordinary occasions would be replaced by a specialist, whose skill was equalled only by his wastefulness'. There was also the extensive royal retinue to accommodate. Small wonder that, according to Lady Warwick, some hosts economised for a whole year, or alternatively got into debt, so that they might entertain royalty for a single weekend. However, as Jonathan Ruffer notes drily, it was 'usually more comfortable to stay in the home of some nouveau riche' who could provide each guest with his own bathroom than in a more aristocratic but less affluent stately home with few modern amenities.

LUNCH.

OLD STYLE.   NEW STYLE.

On major shooting days the 'guns' might have as many as two or three loaders apiece to maintain the flow of firearms. On less important days, only one loader would be needed. These men were usually drawn from the household, perhaps normally working as footmen or gardeners, but sometimes the sportsmen brought their own loaders. The object was to ensure the front man was always 'fed' with a loaded weapon. Beaters were recruited, too, sometimes numbering as many as sixty or eighty at a single shoot. They were often dressed in distinctive white smocks, perhaps with a red collar and a red band on their hats, to make them visible to the guns, as well as to protect their clothing from thorns and bushes. By dressing them

As game preservation increased in popularity and more and more of the nouveaux riches were attracted to it, so shooting lunches became increasingly luxurious in the later Victorian years (Punch, 1882).

A SHOOTING PARTY AT WILTON HOUSE

Among those in the group are the Earl of Pembroke, Lord Ingestre, Lord Herbert, Captain Cook, Lord Hyde, Mr. Napper, the Hon. George Herbert. Lady Muriel Herbert is on horseback behind the group

A shooting party at Wilton House, home of the Earl of Pembroke (The Tatler, 25 September 1901).

A gamekeeper showing dissatisfaction at his paltry tip (Punch, 1882).

DIAGNOSIS.

Keeper. "There!—I thought he worn't a Ge'tleman! 'Shoots 'ith Brown Cartridges, and on'y gi' me 'Alf-a-Crown!"

in a distinctive outfit it was possible to show, too, that they were authorised participants in the shoot, rather than simply hangers on.

On certain estates gratuities were handed to the head keeper by members of the shooting party at the end of the day, and these would subsequently be shared out among members of the regular staff.

Apart from their leisure aspects, hunting, shooting and fishing had important economic implications too, with hard-hit landlords renting or selling sporting rights to wealthy businessmen. After the death of the 8th Duke of Argyll, even Inveraray Castle was let to strangers for a time, and by the final quarter of the nineteenth

A keeper encountering a fisherman who was defying the conventions of the sport (Punch, 1885).

"IN FLAGRANTE."

Keeper (coming on him unawares). "Do you call this Fishing with a Fly, Sir!"
Brigson. "Eh?—I ah well, I—Look here—have a—(*Diving for his flask*)—take a n'p?—Do!!"   [*Tableau!*

century new owners controlled about 70 per cent of the mainland and the insular parishes of western Argyll, Inverness and Ross: 'The shooting box and the fishing lodge were now potential items in every plutocrat's portfolio.'

In 1865, William Cunliffe Brooks, a Lancashire banker, rented Drummond Castle in Perthshire for the shooting. The snobbish housekeeper was not very happy, considering him impossibly vulgar and referring to him behind his back as 'Mr Snooks'. But Cunliffe Brooks was in no way deterred and he subsequently purchased two Scottish estates – Aboyne Castle in 1888 and the Glen Tanar property in Aberdeen in 1891. He had previously leased them from the spendthrift Marquess of Huntly. Around the end of the century T. H. Mawson, who was engaged by Cunliffe Brooks as a landscape gardener, described the daily routine at Glen Tanar: 'Promptly at seven o'clock in the morning the piper's wail began … At ten minutes past a footman came with a cup of tea, informing you that your bath was ready; … breakfast at 7.45; prayers at 8.20.' Most of the guests then went out fishing or shooting. After dinner each evening, the gillies deposited 'in the dining room the kill of the day, whether of rod or gun, and the company rose ceremoniously, inspecting the kill, paid compliments, and heard comparisons from Bailey, the head gillie.'

It was in such circumstances that in 1882 Charles Milnes Gaskell observed that Scotland was being overrun during the shooting season, 'not by English squires, for they have not the means, but by wealthy stockbrokers, by the heads of large establishments in London, by the owners of funded property'. It was symptomatic of the trend that from the 1880s until 1914, the London & North Western Railway provided a special service to cater for the sportsmen during the shooting season. It took the form of 'a horse and carriage special, overnight, from Euston to Inverness'.

An advertisement for shooting clothes to be worn on the moors during inclement weather (The Field, 3 October 1885).

POOR CREATURE!

Nurse. "WELL, MR. CHARLES, HOW DO *YOU* GET ON IN THE COUNTRY ?"
Mr. Charles. "WHY, HEMMA, I SHAN'T BE SORRY WHEN WE RETURNS TO TOWN. I AIN'T A SPORTIN' MAN, YOU KNOW; AND THERE'S NO SOCIETY HERE BUT FISHIN' AND SHOOTIN' !"

Servants who accompanied their masters to shooting parties did not always relish the experience (Punch, 1868).

Chapter Five

THE LONDON SEASON AND OTHER PLEASURES

MOST OF THE LARGER landowners possessed more than one stately home, as well as a London house, which they owned or merely rented for the Season. They might also have a hunting or shooting box for sporting purposes and some took lodgings at the seaside during the summer to benefit their children. Inevitably this meant households were frequently on the move, although a small number of servants — usually a housekeeper, one or two housemaids, and members of the outdoor staff — would be left behind as cleaners and caretakers when the family moved on. The rest of the indoor servants went with them and were, indeed, expected largely to manage the whole procedure. That included arranging for the safekeeping of any plate left behind and opening up the new house in readiness for the arrival of the master and mistress. Stanley Sewell, who worked for a Surrey landowner, particularly enjoyed the time spent in Scotland. This lasted from August, when grouse shooting and deer stalking began, until early October. As second footman, he went up a week in advance to get all the silver ready for use and make other preparations. When his employer and guests went out shooting Stanley served their luncheon in the open air. But what he liked best was the greater informality: 'you didn't have to be so polite and bow and scrape so.'

John James, first footman to the Countess of Camperdown in the mid-1890s, recalled that his mistress spent six months of the year in the country and about six months in London. In the interval between the moves she went to Droitwich for three weeks to take the brine baths, while her household got things in order. She took with her to Droitwich her lady's maid and James, who took the opportunity to sample the hot brine baths himself.

Again, when Lord Salisbury engaged a new tutor for his sons he pointed out that about five months each year would be spent in London, with the rest of the time divided between Cranborne in Dorset and Hatfield, his principal seat in Hertfordshire. From October to February they were based at Hatfield, where Saturday to Monday house parties were frequently held.

It was this multiple occupancy of country estates that led to the 17th Earl of Derby being described as 'a man who had eight houses and no home'. Knowsley, his Lancashire mansion, was the nearest thing he had to a home, but for much of his life he rarely spent more than ten or eleven weeks there. That included a family house party at Christmas and a second house party for members of the racing fraternity to coincide with the running of the Grand National at Aintree. The Dukes of Devonshire had five country houses, in addition to Chatsworth and their London properties.

Opposite:
Guests arriving too early for a ball (1873). Two maids peep round the door to view the early arrivals (James Jacques Joseph Tissot, 1836–1902). (Guildhall Art Gallery/The Bridgeman Art Library)

THE COUNTY BALL.

Above:
A reception at an evening party during the London Season. (The Robert Opie Collection)

Right:
Country-house parties were an integral part of the social scene for landed families. This group at Luton Hoo in the mid-1880s included, standing on the far left, the mistress of the house, Mme de Falbe, holding a parasol. On her left is the Duchess of Teck, mother of Princess Mary of Teck, the future Queen Mary. She is seated on the far left of the garden seat. (Luton Museum and Art Gallery)

*The Duchess of Wellington's Garden Party at Apsley House in London during July 1901 (*The Tatler, *17 July 1901).*

The fact that these grandees were linked by marriage to a number of other leading families meant that uncles, aunts and cousins came to stay for days or weeks at a time in what one writer has called 'great gatherings of the clan'. But feuds and tensions could also arise when family members had to spend so much time in one another's company. Then a prolonged visit to friends might offer a welcome diversion.

Underlying these migrations was an accepted pattern of social activities. Families went to London in April or May for the Season, unless they were involved in parliamentary affairs, in which case they would return to the capital in February for the new session. At the end of July many went to Cowes for the yachting, after which some travelled abroad or went to the seaside, and others returned to the country or migrated to Scotland for the sport. The Christmas period would usually be spent at their principal seat, and after that there would perhaps be a trip abroad. All of this would be interspersed with visits to other country houses. William Lanceley served one couple as a footman and went with them to many house parties. As a consequence he travelled 'from the North of Scotland to the South of England and visited some of the best houses in the country. In those days visiting

A summer boating excursion on the Conway *from Park Place, Remenham Hill, near Henley, c. 1898. (Images and Voices, Oxfordshire County Council)*

HOW THE LUGGAGE IS LOST.

Lady's-Maid. "THOMAS, WHY DON'T YOU SEE THE BOXES PUT IN THE VAN? THEY MAY BE LOST!"
Thomas. "I'M NOT GOING TO TROUBLE MYSELF WITH ALL THAT THERE LUGGAGE. IT'S THE PORTER'S BUSINESS. HE'S PAID FOR IT!"

servants were asked to wait at table … A dress suit did not take up much space in my kit, besides there was sometimes a tip from the host for the work.' He stayed with this couple for two years.

Landowners with more than one property ensured they visited each of them at least once a year so as to maintain their political and social influence in the surrounding area as well as to check on the running of the estate. These tours of inspection were arranged as far as possible to coincide with political or sporting events, or to enable other interests to be pursued, so that business was combined with pleasure.

Lord Ernest Hamilton described country-house parties as 'shut off from the outside world', with those participating enjoying themselves singing, dancing, flirting, shooting, hunting and fishing 'in a little self-contained kingdom, of which the host and hostess were the undisputed king and queen.' Elinor Glyn, writing of the 1890s, also recalled the romantic encounters that were a feature of many country-house gatherings: 'Men did all the chasing … By the end of the first evening you usually knew which member of the party intended to make it his business to amuse you – in a discreet way – during the rest of the visit, in the hope of who knows what reward?' But, she emphasised, however pleasant these flirtations might be, '*there must be no scandal*'. For in those circles divorce or even separation meant social ostracism, especially for the women involved.

A family on the move. Punch drew attention to the arrogant footman and an anxious lady's maid, worried that her employers' luggage would be lost (1875).

During dreary autumn and winter months, house parties enabled people to meet and enjoy themselves, to counter the dark days and gloom outside. In early December 1860, for example, the Spencers spent several days as guests of the Cowpers at Wrest Park in Bedfordshire. There were walks in the garden and the pleasure grounds during the day, dances in the evening, and preparations made for the playing of charades. On 12 December, there was dancing followed by a game of musical chairs, which Charlotte Spencer called 'Mufti':

> [I]t went on till Spencer & I remained the sole proprietors of the only 2 chairs there were … then one was removed & Spencer won – one's crinoline being a sad drawback in this game. After Mufti we valsed again – then a Sir Roger de Coverley – wh[ich] merged into a galop [*sic*] – the galop into a perpetual Jig & finally God Save the Queen was played, Lady Cowper [the hostess] was put into a great Chair – & we marched two and two – curtseying … as we passed her. Then 3 cheers were given for Lady Cowper & … 3 for Mr Oakes the Pianist who had grown white under his prolonged exertions – at last at 3 o C[lock] we proceeded upstairs to bed, cheered by the Gentlemen till we had disappeared from view … Never were people more mad than we were that evening … a cool looker on fresh

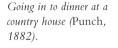

Going in to dinner at a country house (Punch, *1882).*

A GALLANT REPLY.

Miss Lucy. "HERE 'S WHERE YOU AND I ARE TO SIT, MAJOR!"
The Major. "BY JOVE!—A—RATHER A WARM PLACE!"

Miss Lucy. "WHAT—YOU A MAJOR, AND CAN'T STAND FIRE!"
The Major. "NOT AT MY BACK, YOU KNOW, MISS LUCY!"

to the scene must have thought us a set of lunatics – Such is the power of music & the inspiriting effect of dancing!

Musical entertainment as depicted by James Jacques Joseph Tissot, c. 1875. (Manchester Art Gallery / The Bridgeman Art Library)

Two days later there was a meet of the local hunt at Wrest Park and Spencer rode out with them, while Charlotte and some of the others walked in the grounds. However, both Spencers left Wrest Park for Althorp later in the day. On her arrival home Charlotte confessed that she was 'not sorry to have complete rest after so much racketting'. But then she added somewhat wistfully that 'it is rather flat after all the excitement we have had lately … One reason it was so pleasant, added to everybody being good natured & willing to be amused … [was] a beautiful hall to dance in & a charming suite of rooms to sit in – with comfortable fires … if one did not wish to dance.'

However, not all those attending house parties found them enjoyable. Benjamin Disraeli, who went for political and social reasons, fell into this category, as he climbed 'the greasy pole' to become Prime Minister. He had little interest in the sporting activities that were central to many such gatherings, and he described Sundays at a country house as 'infernal'. 'For Disraeli,' writes Sarah Bradford, 'insensible to the delights of shooting five hundred birds a day, still less in hearing of them afterwards, the tedium was dreadful.' According to his wife, whenever they went to a country house, 'the same thing happens: Disraeli is not only bored, and has constant ennui, but he takes on eating as a resource: he eats at breakfast, luncheon

Henley Royal Regatta, c. 1877, was an event that formed part of the social scene during the London Season (James Jacques Joseph Tissot, 1836–1902). (The Bridgeman Art Library)

and dinner: the result is, by the end of the third day he becomes dreadfully bilious; and we have to come away.' Disraeli himself wryly defined country-house visiting as 'a succession of meals relieved by the dresses of the ladies.'

For hostesses, too, house parties could prove unattractive if the company were invited for reasons of duty rather than friendship. At Eaton, Lady Elizabeth Grosvenor particularly disliked the frequent appearance of the Miss Luxmoores. They were the elderly daughters of a bishop and on one occasion she complained to her mother because those 'vile harpies the Miss Luxmoores – vulgar and detestable in every way' had arrived the previous day. That morning they had gone to inspect one of the local schools, where she expected them to 'punish, exhort, examine and condemn the miserable children and frightened schoolmaster and mistresses'. Fortunately most of the Eaton guests were more congenial. Although during the day she and her lady visitors spent many hours walking in the garden, going for drives, or sitting at their needlework while they gossiped, the evenings were enlivened with dancing, cards, billiards, games and charades. Lady Elizabeth thoroughly enjoyed all this. Once she reported 'dancing country dances and polonnaises and playing round games till 1 in the morning – had great fun.' Charades were her particular favourite, these having become popular in stately homes during the mid-1820s as alternatives to amateur theatricals and musical evenings, which could be of very variable quality.

During these migrations the servants who accompanied families were able to meet colleagues from other households and to exchange news and perhaps details of possible staff vacancies. The merits and deficiencies of individual employers were discussed, and the extra-marital misdoings and misdeeds of masters and mistresses recounted with relish. George Cornwallis-West claimed that when a friend asked his valet how the servants amused themselves below stairs in the evenings during a house party, the man admitted that one of their 'favourite amusements' was 'piecing together the letters found in the wastepaper baskets in the morning – better than any jigsaw puzzle, I can assure your lordship – more entertaining'. Ladies' maids and valets learned many of their employers' most intimate secrets. Hence when Lady Warwick had an illicit abortion in France early in the twentieth century, after an extra-marital affair with the socialite Joe Laycock, it was her lady's maid, Helena Clarke, who acted as her nurse and confidante. Lady Warwick had already had one son by Laycock and was later to give birth to his daughter. On one occasion Helena told a friend of Lady Warwick that she had had to 'soothe my lady like a child'.

Less controversial than these activities, however, were the dances and parties held for the servants in some country houses. At Longleat, these were organised twice a week, on Tuesdays and Thursdays, in the servants' hall. A pianist was engaged from nearby Warminster, and a buffet supper was provided by the kitchen and still room staff. The outdoor servants attended, too, and the housekeeper kept a strict eye on the younger maids to make sure they did not behave too frivolously with the unmarried grooms and gardeners. Elsewhere sporting facilities were provided for the men servants. Charles Cooper, when butler to Mr Wingfield of Ampthill House, remembered male members of staff playing cricket and football. Cooper eventually organised an estate cricket team, with fixtures arranged with other clubs in the locality.

The amount of free time enjoyed by servants depended often on the level of entertaining that took place. When George Slingsby went as a hall boy to Rufford Abbey in the early 1900s the housekeeper told him that his duties would begin at

The entertaining of guests could be a problem for country-house hostesses (Punch, 1885).

MUSIC AT HOME. (IN THE COUNTRY HOUSE.)

Herr Bémolski (by request). "ACH, IF YOUR LATYSHIP SHALL CRACIOUSLY BERMIT, I SHALL BLAY FOR YOU MY RONTO ANTANTINO GABRICCIOSO IN F MOLL!"

Noble Hostess. "OH, THAT WILL BE *VERY* NICE! I'M AFRAID THE PIANO IS NOT IN FIRST-RATE ORDER, BY THE BYE. OUR TUNER DIED A FEW YEARS AGO, AND WE'VE NEVER BEEN ABLE TO *FIND ANOTHER!*"

6 o'clock each morning but there would be 'no set working hours'. When the family entertained he might be on call until midnight. However, he would have one weekend off every month and one other free day each fortnight. Formal holidays lasting for several days were more of a problem. According to William Lanceley, he had his first holiday in one household after four years' service when the family went away on a series of visits due to last six weeks. But 'no servant would dream of asking for one unless the family were away from home'. His first break lasted three days but he thought that quite sufficient: 'Our cottage homes and food were no comparison to what we had left behind', though most servants welcomed the opportunity to see their parents and brothers and sisters once more.

For many landed families, however, it was the London Season that was the central point of their social year. Its importance lay in the way it brought together the country's leaders for social, political and match-making purposes. Active political figures returned to the capital in February, when Parliament resumed, but for most members of High Society the Season proper began two or three months later. Lady Randolph Churchill claimed that between October and February London was a social desert, but that had changed by 1 May:

Belgravia … would open the doors of its freshly-painted and flower-bedecked mansions. Dinners, balls, and parties succeeded one another

Spectators at Henley Royal Regatta, c. 1898. (Images and Voices, Oxfordshire County Council)

without intermission till the end of July, the only respite being at the Whitsuntide [parliamentary] recess.

Balls and dinner parties were held, these including about five or six different courses but extending to as many as eight or ten courses on special occasions. This put particular pressure on the kitchen staff. The theatre, the opera and exhibitions were patronised, with the Gaiety Theatre favoured by some of the young bloods. Sporting events, such as pigeon shooting and polo at Hurlingham and Ranelagh, race meetings, and cricket matches at Lord's were other features of the Season. In July there was the Henley Royal Regatta and then came racing at Goodwood and yachting at Cowes.

The young Consuelo Marlborough recalled her first London Season in the 1890s as 'a pageant … a stately ritual … I was impressed by the splendour of the receptions I attended. The stately homes in which they were given had a lordly air … We dined out nearly every night and there were always parties, often several, in the evening. Indeed one had to exercise discretion in one's acceptances in order to survive the three months season.' There were other rituals to be observed, too, such as riding in Rotten Row in the morning, where 'we … looked our best in classic riding-habits', and in the evening driving 'slowly back and forth in stately barouches' in Hyde Park, 'elaborately bedecked in ruffles and lace'.

Rotten Row, Hyde Park, London.

At the heart of this whirl of social activity were the Prince and Princess of Wales and their 'Marlborough House set', so named after their official London residence. Lady Warwick, who had a close relationship with the Prince during the 1890s, remembered a 'special achievement' of the Marlborough House set was 'to turn night into day. We would dine late and long, trifle with the Opera for an hour or so, or watch the ballet at the Empire, then "go on" to as many houses as we could crowd in.'

But the Treasury official and man-about-town Sir Edward Hamilton viewed the Prince's participation with a less indulgent eye. In his diary on 24 May 1887, Hamilton noted that he had attended a ball given by Mrs Oppenheim:

> … whose entertainments are always most pleasant and well done – The Prince of Wales was there (one might add, as usual): for there is hardly a Ball now with any pretensions to smartness which he not only attends but at which he remains till a very late hour. This is scarcely dignified at his age. His capacity for amusing himself is extraordinary; he is able to get on with hardly any sleep.

The Prince's mother, Queen Victoria, shared these reservations. As early as 1868 she had written to Benjamin Disraeli, then serving briefly as Prime Minister, commenting acidly that '*any encouragement*' to the Prince's 'constant love of moving about, and not keeping at home … is most *earnestly* … to be deprecated.'

Rotten Row, Hyde Park, was the place to be seen by the socially ambitious during the London Season.

Playing billiards in a private house. (The Robert Opie Collection)

During the Season many of the menfolk attended one or other of the London clubs and here, too, the Prince played a prominent role. He was a founder of the Marlborough Club in 1869, when the committee at White's, one of the old established clubs, refused to relax what he regarded as its unreasonable restrictions on smoking. Members of the Marlborough were only admitted with his approval, and apart from such customary facilities as a billiard room it also had a skittle alley. A spirit of lightheartedness prevailed, with the Prince and his friends engaging in gambling and practical jokes. Benjamin Disraeli described these intimates disapprovingly as the 'Marlborough Club banditti'.

The Prince of Wales was a keen gambler, particularly favouring baccarat, which was illegal in Britain. In July 1889 his enthusiasm for the game brought him into conflict with the Duke of Richmond, with whom he was staying for the Goodwood race meeting. According to Sir Edward Hamilton, the Duke objected to baccarat being played in his house:

> contrary to his wishes, implied if not directly expressed, the Royal Party would not refrain from indulging in the game. Though they called it by some other name, he was not to be taken in; & he came down upon the Prince not without some loss of temper, expressing surprise that H.R.H.

should have had the bad taste to resort to gambling in his House. The Prince was extremely annoyed … and declared he would never set foot in the House again. However, on the morrow when the party broke up, both parties cooled down, the Duke apologizing for any excess of warmth he had displayed and the Prince admitted that he had been in the wrong.

In January of the following year, Winifred Sturt, a daughter of Lord Alington, similarly complained to her fiancé about the way in which baccarat was played at Sandringham into the early hours. 'I think it is a shocking affair', she wrote, 'for the Royal Family to play an illegal game every night. They have a real table, and rakes, and everything like the rooms at Monte Carlo.' In the early 1890s the Prince's involvement in the game was to bring him unwelcome publicity and forthright criticism in the press.

During the 1880s the nouveaux riches entered London Society in increasing numbers and were tacitly encouraged so to do by the Prince of Wales. They included wealthy businessmen and financiers as well as a new breed of South African mining millionaires, some of whom were Jewish in origin. There was a note of anti-Semitism in certain of the comments made about them by more established members of society. Lady Warwick, for example, admitted that she and her friends 'resented the introduction of the Jews into the social set of the Prince of Wales', not, she hastily added, because 'we disliked them individually' but because they had brains and as a class 'we did not like brains'. Lord Carrington, in a diary entry during July 1900, was far blunter in his hostility, noting that he had been at a dinner party where Sir Julius Wernher, 'the S. African Jew Millionaire & a flashy painted wife'

A ladies' archery contest in Regent's Park, London, in 1902.

were fellow guests. 'The way London Society toadies these S. African German Jews is horrible. They are subsidizing half London and the women take their beastly money as greedily as the men.' Yet despite such private prejudices, because these men were welcomed by the Prince of Wales, those who aspired to be at the centre of the capital's social round had little choice but to accept them with as good a grace as they could muster.

For the servants, meanwhile, the pressure of the London Season, with its relentless round of parties and balls, was extremely tiring. Eric Horne, when employed as a footman by a master he labelled 'The Bold Bad Baron', remembered the wide range of duties. 'There is not only the day work, but the night work as well. They would keep us out regularly till one, two, or three o'clock, but we had to start work at the same time as the other servants.' When the 'Baron' went out to dinner or another

A lady attended by two footmen about to enter her carriage – part of the ceremonial of service associated with the London Season.

function, he 'always had two footmen standing up behind his … carriage, and the coachman with his curly wig on'. Sometimes Horne was so tired that he fell asleep on the carriage, only to be awakened by the coachman drawing 'the handle of his knotty whip under my nose'. When a ball was held, the footmen were on duty to receive guests at the door, as well as helping with the buffet and making regular inspections to ensure that the oil lamps and candles were burning brightly. 'The Baron', wrote Horne, 'was fond of pomp and show, and liked to see his dress liveries walking about. About four o'clock in the morning it was all over. Then the clearing up began: by the time that was done it was time to begin the ordinary day's work, after we had changed our clothes. This is where that patent handle is wanted to wind servants up, to work on again for another fifteen hours.' The opportunity to earn tips when these major entertainments were held did not always compensate for the extra work involved.

At the end of the Season some country-house families travelled abroad for pleasure or for health reasons. Lady Warwick noted ruefully that: 'Nerves, indigestion, sometimes plain obesity, due to too many meals and too little exercise,' made it necessary to seek a 'cure at a foreign spa … and London society was compelled to visit such places as Homburg, Marienbad, or Wiesbaden.' The Prince of Wales at this time favoured Homburg and he was followed there by other members of his social

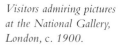

Visitors admiring pictures at the National Gallery, London, c. 1900.

The 5th Earl of Warwick in the 1890s, when his wife was enjoying the company of a number of admirers, including the Prince of Wales.

circle. 'Wonderful balls were given at Homburg for the Prince', recalled Lady Warwick. The taking of baths, the drinking of large quantities of spa water, a restricted diet, and plenty of walks in the surrounding countryside were part of the recommended regimen. But the wealthy socialites who met there and exchanged gossip also wore their smartest clothes and attended concerts, as well as making excursions into the countryside. The Countess of Fingall, who went to Bad Schwalbach in 1897, recalled nostalgically the meals out of doors among the flowers, since although she was supposed to be 'doing the cure' the food was delicious.

For those with a delicate constitution, winters in the south of France were increasingly attractive, although some families chose to travel to Egypt or the Canary Islands. Switzerland, too, gained in popularity at the end of the century with the growth of winter sports. The French Riviera, however, proved particularly popular, with Nice offering the men clubs, casinos and cafés while the women engaged in visits to their friends and preparations for balls and parties. There were regattas, too, in which the Prince of Wales took part.

Servants might share in these overseas visits, too. Indeed, valets travelling with their master were expected to decipher train timetables and to act as couriers and interpreters when they were abroad. In 1873, when the 4th Lord Carnarvon engaged a new valet, it was noted that one of the merits of the chosen candidate was that he could order 'anything in French'.

In 1900 the Mullhollands of Beccles in Suffolk were attended by twelve of their permanent staff when they rented a villa in Cannes for three months. For some of the younger servants it was their first trip abroad. One junior Mullholland maid recalled that her face was a 'shining light' as she made a brief tour of Paris on the journey south. Charles Cooper had several trips to the Riviera. Once his employers stayed at an hotel near Menton where before they left the management gave a 'Couriers Ball' for the servants who had been staying with their masters and mistresses in the hotel. Cooper found it all 'most enjoyable'.

Several aristocrats bought their own villas in France or Italy. In 1870 Lord Salisbury purchased a property on the cliffs at Puys near Dieppe. A quarter of a century later he sold it and built a new house near Monte Carlo. In 1897 Lord Rosebery acquired a villa near Naples. Egypt, too, from the 1880s became a favoured destination for those seeking winter warmth and an exotic landscape. Earl Spencer wintered there in February 1899, visiting Luxor, Abu Simbel, Assouan and Cairo, as well as making certain political contacts. He and the Countess then travelled on to Italy, where they visited Pompeii and Rome.

Visitors at Bad Ems in Germany parading in the park while following the example of the Prince of Wales by taking a 'cure' at a continental spa.

For the most opulent or adventurous grandees, ownership of a seagoing yacht proved attractive. Lord Rosebery and Lord Carnarvon both spent much time sailing among the islands of the Aegean. More modestly, the widowed Emily Meynell Ingram, who had estates in Staffordshire and Yorkshire, was an enthusiastic yachtswoman. For eleven years from 1886 she was the proud owner of the *Ariadne*, a 360-ton yacht, with a full-time crew of around thirty. Twice a year she and some friends spent up to two or three months cruising in the Mediterranean during the early spring and venturing to Scandinavia and the Baltic during the summer.

For families with children, seaside holidays in England were often the order of the day. Members of the Wrey and Wilder families at Shanklin on the Isle of Wight, c. 1898. The young nursemaid on the left of the photograph is sitting bolt upright. (Museum of English Rural Life, University of Reading)

It was in these circumstances that Lady Dorothy Nevill contrasted the lifestyle of some major landed families and nouveaux riches early in the twentieth century with that during her early Victorian youth:

> Half a century ago a rich man … was quite content to live the greater part of the year on his estate … What is the life of the rich man of to-day? A sort of firework! Paris, Monte Carlo, big-game shooting in Africa, fishing in

A family holiday at home, as portrayed by William Holman Hunt (1827– 1900). (Tor Abbey / The Bridgeman Art Library)

Norway, dashes to Egypt, trips to Japan ... He has, of course, a house in town, but so busy is he that as often as not he is too hurried to go there ... Such individuals have changed the whole standard of living, and imported the bustle of the Stock Exchange into the drawing-rooms of Mayfair.

Yet, if this was the experience of a number of important stately-home owners, it must be remembered that many less affluent members of the gentry, like the Yorkes of Erddig or the Shiffners of Combe Place, Hamsey in Sussex, enjoyed far simpler pleasures. For the Yorkes, there were musical evenings at home or visits to friends in the locality and occasional lengthier stays with relatives. They never visited London for the Season. Similarly Lady Elizabeth Shiffner and her daughters found most of their amusements in their locality, notably in nearby Lewes and in Brighton, as well as in the neighbouring villages. The girls were enthusiastic sportswomen, with the two youngest keen women cricketers and tennis players during the summer, and riders to hounds in the winter. On 3 August 1887, for example, Lady Elizabeth and her daughters went to a circus at Lewes. The next day they attended a 'Married & Single Ladies' Cricket' match; and the day after that, while two of the girls played tennis, Lady Shiffner dined with friends. Later there was a garden party at the home of another friend and a visit to Tunbridge Wells Show. Occasional holidays were taken in Devon and the Isle of Wight, and there were brief visits to the homes of relatives and friends. The Shiffners rarely went to London and when they did it was for business and shopping rather than to follow the social round.

It is worth stressing the limited horizons of these many modest landed families when considering the extravagant pastimes and pleasures enjoyed by the major grandees during the Victorian and Edwardian years.

Amateur theatricals were a popular feature at many country-house parties. A group of friends at Wakehurst Place performing The Merchant of Venice *in the early 1900s.*

Chapter Six

THE END OF AN ERA

DURING the twentieth century and particularly since the Second World War, the economic, political and even social role of the country house and its owners has steadily diminished. In 1974, James Lees-Milne lamented the speed with which this 'revolution' was taking place. It had taken, he wrote, 'a mere lifetime to wipe out an institution of four centuries ... [The] First World War gravely shook the foundations. The Second World War toppled it. Subsequent social trends have brought it crashing to the ground.' Paramount among the causes of this, in his view, were the effects of penal rates of taxation, an inability to recruit sufficient domestic staff, and the fact that 'the spirit of the age [was] against what is termed "privilege".'

In reality, however, the undermining of the country-house way of life had begun some decades earlier, during the late Victorian years, for those landowners who depended on income from agriculture and farm rentals for their support. From the late 1870s poor harvests in Britain and the effects of cheap food imports had led to a fall in agricultural prosperity, with some tenant farmers either giving up their holdings because they could no longer make a profit by running them, or demanding – and receiving – substantial rent rebates and reductions from their landlord. Although the impact of declining rentals varied according to the kind of farming carried on (those in dairying areas did not see their income diminish in the way that grain producers did), the general trend was downwards. That continued into the early twentieth century, with some landlords seeing their income halved. At the same time the tax burden was increasing, with a new estates duty imposed from 1894, payable on the death of the owner, and with the burden of income tax also increasing.

In these circumstances hard-hit stately-home owners sought to reduce their expenditure or to sell or lease part of their estate to the nouveaux riches. Others decided to forgo or restrict the pleasures of the London Season, or to cut their expenditure on domestic staff and on their sporting activities. The greater use of motor cars meant fewer men were needed in the stables, while the increased availability of commercial laundries permitted the closure of many country house laundries, or their replacement by daily washerwomen.

Particularly affected were gentry families who had few alternative resources but their land on which to rely. At Cranmer Hall in Norfolk during the 1890s the Jones family, according to one of their sons, were much concerned by the low rents, the need for rent remittances and the losses that arose from the running of the home farm. As a consequence, economy became the order of the day. 'One by one, the laundry was closed, the footman left, and after him the groom; Mr Basham retired from the garden and was not replaced; my father's riding-horse was sold.' Significantly, even when his father had inherited the estate it was already burdened with a bank overdraft and mortgages.

Opposite:
A touch of modernity.
Lady Warwick behind the
wheel of a car in 1902,
accompanied by her second
son, Maynard.

The increasing importance of motor cars as
the preferred means of transport for the
well-to-do became very evident. Chauffeurs
outside the garages at Pusey House, Pusey,
c. 1900. The larger car has a luggage rack.
(Images and Voices, Oxfordshire County
Council)

King Edward VII's first experience as a
motorist around the beginning of the 1900s
at Highcliffe Castle, then in Hampshire.

116

Another gentry family badly affected by the depression was the Knightleys of Fawsley Hall in Northamptonshire. When Lord Knightley died in 1895 mortgage interest and rent charges exceeded the annual yield from estate rentals. This meant that until her death in 1913 his widow was under continuous financial pressure. Servants were dismissed, so that by 1901 she employed only six female and two male staff indoors compared to the fourteen at work a decade earlier. Letting the house for brief periods was another strategy she adopted to make ends meet, although she much disliked it. As early as 1901 she was shocked to receive a letter from the bank telling her 'in peremptory terms that I *must* retrench somewhere and I must resolve to limit the hospitality I so much enjoy'. Louisa Knightley was the last member of the family to reside at Fawsley, after a continuous occupation for almost five centuries. In May 1914 the contents of the Hall were sold and after the death of Lord Knightley's heir in 1932, the house fell into disrepair. In 1948 it became a factory for timber products, and it was only in the 1980s that restoration work was carried out. By 1998 it had become an hotel.

Some larger landowners experienced difficulties, too, so that at Althorp Earl Spencer was forced to give up the Mastership of the Pytchley Hounds in 1894 on financial grounds, and to reduce his domestic staff. In 1892, after much deliberation, he decided to sell the valuable Althorp library to a Manchester purchaser, Mrs John Rylands, for around £250,000. Even then he had to warn his wife in January 1894 of the need to cut expenditure further. 'We shall have to keep every cost down this year very sharp.'

Other landowners, too, disposed of valuable assets in order to continue their traditional lifestyle as far as possible. At Blenheim Palace between 1881 and 1883 the famous library collected by the 3rd Earl of Sunderland was sold by the Duke of Marlborough.

A visit by King Edward VII to Blenheim Palace at the beginning of the twentieth century. (Images and Voices, Oxfordshire County Council)

The 1880s also saw the auctioning of books from libraries at Stourhead and Osterley Park among others. Elsewhere owners like Lord Tweedmouth disposed of valuable art collections.

For others again the solution was to move out of the main house, leaving it empty or letting it where possible, and to reside in a smaller property. At Savernake the 5th Marquess of Ailesbury succeeded in 1894 to a much-neglected estate, and resolved to live in a smaller house within its boundaries, leaving his major seat, Tottenham Park, empty. The game and the deer were made self-supporting by increasing the sales of birds and venison and by a widespread letting of the shooting. Nonetheless, a bank overdraft was needed to keep the estate going.

A number of owners, like Lord Elcho at Stanway in Gloucestershire, embarked on a series of petty economies. However, according to his daughter, Cynthia Charteris, at least part of his problems arose from his addiction to gambling. During her youth in the 1890s there was 'always talk of the necessity for "retrenchment"', even though an ample staff of servants was maintained and the house was 'almost continuously full of visitors'. The economies made took the form of such minor changes as the purchase of third-rate horses, while the family always travelled third class on the railway, except for Lord Elcho himself. He continued to go first class. Heating in the bedrooms at Stanway was kept to a minimum and both Lady Elcho and her daughters spent little on clothes.

Some of the major figures like the Duke of Devonshire, the Duke of Norfolk and Lord Londonderry benefited from alternative sources of income, such as receipts from urban ground rents, earnings from industrial and commercial businesses, and mineral royalties, particularly coal and iron. These before 1914 were immensely lucrative for landowners fortunate enough to have them. Others, lacking such advantages, supplemented their income by going into the City to take up profitable company directorships, or encouraging younger sons to make a career in the City, rather than following the traditional route of joining the Army, the Church or the legal profession. By 1896, 167 noblemen, or over a quarter of the peerage, held directorships, many in more than one company and with firms with which they had had no prior connection. By 1920, the 4th Lord Brabourne, who was descended from a long-established Kentish family, had become a director of thirteen companies. It was this situation that led Lady Dorothy Nevill to observe acidly in 1906 that there were 'now many scions of noble houses who exhibit nearly as much shrewdness in driving bargains in the City as a South African millionaire himself'.

One obvious source of revenue for hard-hit stately home owners would have been the sale of land but this remained difficult until about 1908. Then, as farming improved, a number of tenant farmers entered the market to purchase their own holdings. Between 1908 and 1914 perhaps 800,000 acres of land were sold. This trend was to be even more pronounced after the First World War, between 1918 and 1922, when it has been

The 9th Duke of Marlborough, husband of Consuelo, took a pessimistic view of the future of the landed interest.

estimated that a quarter of the land of England and Wales changed hands. In Scotland the proportion was probably higher still. It was in these circumstances that in May 1920 *The Times* reported gloomily: 'England is changing hands … Will a profiteer buy it? Will it be turned into a school or an institution?' *Country Life* joined in the lament, commenting on the way the countryside was 'changing from month to month', with the dismemberment of so many estates. The 9th Duke of

Golf became an increasingly popular pastime from the late nineteenth century. (The Robert Opie Collection)

Marlborough himself observed in 1920: 'The old order is doomed.' Typical of the changes taking place was the sale of Compton Verney in 1921 by Lord Willoughby de Broke to Joseph Watson, a soap boiler and racehorse owner. He was created Lord Manton shortly afterwards.

By the mid-1920s, however, the land bubble had burst and after its brief war-time prosperity farming slipped back into recession. The old problems of country-house owners reasserted themselves. Staff cutbacks were again made, and some mistresses, like Lady Horner, employed cheaper parlourmaids to replace butlers and footmen. But for many established families that was a step too far. According to a relative, Lord Arran, 'being very upset after a financial crisis in 1932', declared plaintively to his sister: 'Oh, Esther, the only thing left for us to do is to go abroad with parlourmaids.' That was considered 'absolutely the end'.

The post-1918 period was inevitably overshadowed by the heavy death toll experienced by landed families, with their long military traditions, during the First World War. In all nearly one in five of the peers and their sons under the age of fifty who served in the War were killed. It was this loss, coupled with increasingly heavy taxation, that encouraged the 1918 to 1922 upsurge in land sales. The 1919 Budget, for example, raised death duties on estates valued at £2m or more from 20 per cent to 40 per cent, while other taxes also rose. At Wilton, home of the Earl of Pembroke, income tax, which had taken barely 4 per cent of gross rents before 1914, was by

Servants illicitly enjoying music from a gramophone in this advertisement by His Master's Voice. Gramophones were in use from the 1890s.

"His Master's Voice"
or why the dinner was late.

Tea in the garden of Lythanger, home of the Seymour family, in the early twentieth century – an indication of the continuity of country-house life as well as its changes. (Hampshire Record Office)

1919 taking over a quarter. According to one estimate all direct taxes together – land tax, rates and income tax – had risen from 9 to 30 per cent of the rental at Wilton. Most landowners were similarly affected, and it was on these grounds that Lady Newton of Lyme Park in Cheshire complained in 1925 of the dilemma faced by people like herself. She had come as a bride to Lyme in 1880, when the prestige of the landed elite had been at its height. Already between 1919 and 1921, 3,000 acres of agricultural land had been sold from Lyme, and in 1920 the 2nd Lord Newton transferred the estate to his son to avoid the high cost of death duties. Hence Lady Newton's lament in 1925:

> And what of the stately homes of England? … Why … should we be prevented from enjoying our homes that have come down to us from our forefathers? We only demand the right to live in them, without the amenities of former days, but this is to be denied us. What are we to do? We cannot sell, there are no buyers. We cannot afford to live in our homes, what is to become of them?

A few landowners, unable to maintain their properties, took the extreme step of demolishing them. Eglinton Castle in Ayrshire, for example, was unroofed in 1925 and then virtually demolished by being used as target practice on a gunnery range. Hamilton Palace in Strathclyde, owned by the Duke and Duchess of Hamilton and dating back to the seventeenth century, was demolished in 1920. These houses had a number of counterparts south of the border. Drayton Manor, once the home of the Victorian Prime Minister Sir Robert Peel, was demolished in 1926, despite its historic importance. Two years later Norton Priory in Cheshire suffered a similar fate. In addition, several of the grand London houses of leading aristocrats were also destroyed. They included the Duke of Devonshire's impressive Devonshire House

The freedom offered to young people by bicycling is celebrated in this advertisement for Townsend Cycles, c. 1900.

on the north side of Piccadilly, sold for £750,000, so that the site could be redeveloped. As early as 1919, Lord Salisbury had sold his house in Arlington Street, which had been the London home of the Cecil family for generations. In 1928 Dorchester House in Park Lane was sold, demolished, and replaced by an hotel. The disposal of these palatial London dwellings was frequently followed by a sale of the family's art collection that had previously been displayed in them.

During the First World War many country houses had been offered by their owners for use as hospitals or other institutions. At Woburn Abbey, for example, the Riding School was converted to a hospital. But in the Second World War the process was both more systematic and more extensive, with requisitioning taking place on a large scale. After the War, some owners found it impossible to continue in occupation even when the property was returned to them, often damaged by its wartime usage. They could not afford the repairs, and were, in any case, hit by heavy taxes and an inability to recruit, or to afford, sufficient domestic staff. In the 1980s Stanley Sewell, who had spent many years as a butler, claimed that after the War ended in 1945 'you couldn't get men and women for domestic service and you started to get foreign staff as things began to go down. Today I don't think I can name a place in Leicestershire that has two servants.'

Already between 1918 and 1945, more than four hundred country houses had been demolished, while others were redeveloped or converted into schools, hotels, country clubs, conference centres and similar institutions. It was this loss that prompted the passage of legislation in 1937 enabling stately-home owners to donate their property to the National Trust. In return for tax concessions, and, in some cases, continued residence, they gave permission for limited public access by visitors and tourists during the summer months. The scheme proved very successful and whereas in 1939, on the eve of war, only two or three houses had passed to the Trust, by 1974, 110 country houses were in its ownership and numbers have increased thereafter. About half of the 1974 National Trust properties were still inhabited by the donors and their heirs, or by private tenants. Public support for the conservation of country houses helped to boost National Trust membership from 226,000 in 1971 to over a million by the early 1980s. In 2009 it stood at 3.7 million.

Kingston Lacy house in
Dorset: the Spanish room
in 1948. The house was
bequeathed by its last
owner, Ralph Bankes, to
the National Trust on his
death in 1981. The
National Trust formally
accepted ownership in
1983. (English Heritage
Picture Library)

The changing face of the
country house. Cliveden,
home of the Astor family,
c. 1914. In the later
twentieth century it
became an hotel, although
part of it remained open
to members of the public
at limited times, under the
aegis of the National
Trust.

PLEASANT FOR HARRY.

Fair Sportswoman. "OH, HARRY, I FEEL SO EXCITED, I SCARCELY KNOW WHAT I AM DOING!"

Women began to take an active part at shooting parties in the early twentieth century, to the consternation of some of the menfolk (Punch, 1900).

Tax concessions were extended also to private owners who were prepared to open their properties to the public for at least thirty-six days in the year. By the 1950s country-house visiting had become an increasingly popular recreation for many British people, albeit taking place in a very different context from that which had applied to stately homes and their owners in their Victorian heyday. In the early twenty-first century around 700 country houses are open to the public, of which approaching 600 are private properties and most of the rest belong to the National Trust.

The declining economic role of the landed classes was mirrored by their loss of political power as well. No longer did they dominate Parliament, as they had once done, while their role on County Councils or as Justices of the Peace was much eroded. The major grandees continued to enjoy considerable social prestige but even before the Second World War the old way of life had been undermined. 'When I first lived at Welbeck,' wrote the 6th Duke of Portland in 1937, 'the great neighbouring houses … were all inhabited by their owners, who … employed large staffs. Now, not one of them is so occupied, except for a very few days in the year, and the shooting attached to them is either let or abandoned.' The Duke of Windsor in 1953 sounded a similarly mournful note when he commented on the way in which so many homes had

passed under the auctioneer's hammer or been taken over by the National Trust. In many others the squire and his family have retreated perhaps to one of the wings, or to the housekeeper's old quarters, the lodgekeeper's or the gardener's cottage, or in more fortunate circumstances to the dower house. What is left of the shooting has in most cases been let. The retainers – those who have not been pensioned off – have scattered to the factories and farms.

Yet, despite the land sales and the numerous other difficulties, it is worth remembering that many of the largest magnates have remained major owners of country estates. As late as 1976 just 1,500 families owned nearly a third of the rural land of England and Wales. In Scotland the Duke of Buccleuch, with an estate of 220,000 acres, and Lord Seafield, with 213,000 acres, owned the two largest estates in Great Britain at that date. In England in 1976 a major landholder like the Duke of Northumberland had 105,000 acres. However, that was less than two-thirds of what his ancestors had possessed a century earlier.

In modern Britain surviving stately-home owners see themselves as custodians of their land and heritage rather than as leaders of society and arbiters of political and economic policy, either nationally or in the rural communities where they live. Many have introduced commercial ventures on their estates to boost income, perhaps by opening a shop to sell food and garden produce or opening up a theme park. Entrance charges have to be paid by visitors and tea rooms offer them refreshments. This new philosophy was well summarised by the 13th Duke of Bedford in 1959 when he described the innovations he had introduced at Woburn Abbey in an attempt to save the property from dereliction and to pay off the £4.5m in death duties that had been incurred. By 1958 the estate was attracting nearly half a million visitors a year, and the Duke claimed it had 'nearly double the number of visitors to our nearest rival, Chatsworth'. He had adapted his own lifestyle to meet the new situation:

> We run our own wing of Woburn on a very modest scale. Where my grandfather had scores of servants in Belgrave Square and at the Abbey, we make do with seven, … with all the public engagements that the stately-home business entails. We do have fourteen dailies and six night-watchmen who come in on a part-time basis from Woburn village, but their job is to clean and look after the whole vast complex of the house, including the public rooms and the tea-room and restaurant in the stables. We keep no part of the park for ourselves. There are a few notices up marking off sections of it as a private area, but this is chiefly for the protection of the animals, and we expect no further rights in the grounds than we give our visitors. We are perfectly happy to share the pleasures of the estate with them …. I go round the country lecturing, speaking to different societies and trying to interest people who are likely to bring parties during the visiting months …. The best that can be said is that we are nearly breaking even, and that for the moment, at any rate, there is no danger of Woburn falling down from sheer neglect.

*The Hon. Michael Herbert and two of his sons fishing at Wilton House near Salisbury in the early 1900s (*The Tatler*).*

FURTHER READING

Balsan, Consuelo Vanderbilt. *The Glitter and the Gold*. George Mann Books, 1973.

Barstow, Phyllida. *The English Country House Party*. Sutton, 1989.

Bedford, John, Duke of. *A Silver-plated Spoon*. Cassell, 1959.

Crook, J. Mordaunt. *The Rise of the Nouveaux Riches*. J. Murray, 1999.

Gerard, Jessica. *Country House Life: Family and Servants 1815–1914*. Wiley–Blackwell, 1994.

Girouard, Mark. *Life in the English Country House*. Yale University Press, 1979.

Horn, Pamela. *Ladies of the Manor*. Sutton, 1997 edition.

Horn, Pamela. *The Rise and Fall of the Victorian Servant*. Sutton, 2004.

Mulvagh, Jane. *Madresfield: The Real Brideshead*. Doubleday, 2008.

Musgrave, Toby. *The Head Gardeners: Forgotten Heroes of Horticulture*. Aurum, 2007.

Ruffer, Jonathan. *The Big Shots: Edwardian Shooting Parties*. Quiller Press, 1997.

Sambrook, Pamela A. *The Country House Servant*. Sutton, 1999.

Waterson, Merlin (editor). *The Country House Remembered*. Routledge & Kegan Paul, 1985.

Waterson, Merlin. *The Servants' Hall: A Domestic History of Erddig*. Routledge & Kegan Paul, 1980.

INDEX

Page numbers in italics refer to illustrations